BOOKS
A LIVING HISTORY

BOOKS
A LIVING HISTORY

Martyn Lyons

With 266 illustrations, 214 in colour

Thames & Hudson

Contents

Opposite: A wall painting from the Praedia of Julia Felix in Pompeii, depicting Roman writing materials: ink-pot and stylus, papyrus roll and wax tablets. The painting can be found in the National Archaeological Museum, Naples.

Page 1: A plate from Denis Diderot's *Encyclopédie, ou dictionnaire raisonné des sciences, des arts et des métiers*, 1751–72, showing typesetters at work. The 35-volume encyclopaedia illustrated many technological processes of the day.

Page 2: Books lining the walls in American poet Richard Howard's apartment.

First published in the United Kingdom in 2011 by Thames & Hudson Ltd,
181A High Holborn, London WC1V 7QX

First paperback edition 2013

British Library Cataloguing-in-Publication Data
A catalogue record for this book is available from the British Library

ISBN 978-0-500-29115-3

Printed and bound in China by
Toppan Leefung Printing Limited

To find out about all our publications, please visit
www.thamesandhudson.com.
There you can subscribe to our e-newsletter, browse or download our current catalogue, and buy any titles that are in print.

Introduction: The Power and Magic of the Book

The book has proved one of the most useful, versatile and enduring technologies in history. Its portability, ease of reference, and ability to concentrate a large amount of data made it indispensable. It is difficult now to imagine how some of the great turning points in Western history could have been achieved without it. The Renaissance, the Reformation, the Scientific Revolution and the Age of Enlightenment all relied on the printed word for their spread and permanent influence. For two and a half millennia, humanity has used the book, in its manuscript or printed form, to record, to administer, to worship and to educate.

Embattled book lovers often insist that books do not need batteries, they do not get infected by viruses and when you close a book you never need to 'save' because you will never lose your data. The book has always been much more than a useful gadget. Among other things, it can be a pedagogical instrument, a source of religious inspiration and a work of art. It has been the basis of religions and a source of immense political power. Christianity, Judaism and Islam – three of the great religions of the world – are centred around sacred books. Great states and empires everywhere have derived enormous power from written texts that record taxation or outline legal codes and decisions. People who were subjugated by oppressive regimes understood that governments depended on the written word for their authority and bureaucratic operation. 'Let's kill all the lawyers!' cry the Kentish rebels of 1450 in Shakespeare's *Henry VI Part 2*, defending the power of oral tradition against the authorities' books and literate culture. During the French Revolution of 1789, burning written tax records was a popular pastime for peasants in revolt.

Humanity has long attributed magical power to the written word. During the colonization of the Caribbean, for instance, Spanish chronicler Gonzalo Fernández de Oviedo y Valdés (1478–1557) reported that the indigenous people regarded the letters written by their conquerors as supernatural objects: 'it seemed to them that the letter knew what would happen to the recipient; and sometimes a few of the least intelligent among them thought that it had a soul'. In a nineteenth-century account from the Pyrenees recorded by the ethnographer Daniel Fabre, a woman reading *Le Petit Albert*, a popular magic handbook, became possessed by the devil, who took hold of her and paralysed her legs until a pilgrimage to Lourdes cured her. In many traditional societies, books possessed miraculous and symbolic powers that only members of the religious elite knew how to manipulate. If anyone usurped this clerical monopoly over the written word, they risked accusations of heresy, as English Lollards and French Cathars learned at their peril, not to mention the Mayans, whose books were branded as idolatrous and destroyed by their Catholic Spanish conquerors.

The Virgin holds a book in this detail of *The Annunciation*, painted *c.* 1440 by the Flemish Renaissance artist Rogier van der Weyden. The painting is held in the Louvre.

In the West, the Bible had special magical and healing powers. In seventeenth-century England and New England, for instance, it was thought to cure nosebleeds and to protect pregnant women from complications in childbirth. During the late Victorian period, one English woman in Hampshire who suffered from fits reportedly ate an entire New Testament in an attempt to cure her illness, putting each page in the middle of a sandwich. The Bible was also used as an oracle: people dipped into it at random to find a solution for their dilemmas.

In the Père Lachaise cemetery in Paris, there is a striking nineteenth-century tombstone, entirely sculpted in the shape of a book. The pages curl realistically, and the individual leaves are picked out in stone. In Christian cultures good deeds and bad were imagined as recorded in a vast ledger of sin and redemption at the Last Judgment of souls. Woe betide those who did not end up with a credit balance. The book was, in this way, a metaphor for life itself.

Today, however, the book has lost its magical aura and is no longer the indispensable attribute of government. It has become an everyday consumer object, like soap or potatoes. What is more, in the early twenty-first century, we seem to be passing through an information revolution that may irrevocably undermine the status of the book and even – according to the most extreme predictions – render it obsolete. Considering the increasing amount of paper consumed globally, prophecies foretelling the end of paper-based technologies seem absurd. But this is a good moment to take stock, to look back and to consider the book's history and evolution from scribal production to printed page, from large format to the pocket paperback edition, and from the scroll to the codex and the e-book.

In Christianity and Judaism the 'Book of Life' records the names of every person born and their deeds and misdeeds for divine judgment. The idea was taken literally in this tombstone in the shape of a book which can be found in Père Lachaise cemetery in north-eastern Paris.

The Revolutions of the Book

Besides the introduction of the printing press there were other, equally important changes in the history of books and the way men and women read them. One of the first revolutions of the book was the invention of the codex, originating in the Christian world of the second and third centuries, when the book ceased to be a scroll, or *volumen*, and became a collection of separate sheets loosely attached to each other. The codex was a book with pages that turned, instead of a long strip of material that unrolled. Unlike the invention of printing, the codex revolutionized the shape of the book itself, and gave us a material form of the book that lasted for centuries.

A second revolution was the slow transition from oral reading to silent reading. Historians believe that in the ancient world books were read aloud or declaimed to an audience by trained orators. Reading was a performance. In medieval Europe, however, monks gradually began to adopt the practice of silent reading as a form of devotion. For the first time, texts that had previously been produced in completely unbroken script began to acquire rudimentary punctuation and spaces between words. These changes made individual silent reading easier, and permitted less experienced orators to read texts aloud more easily.

The so-called 'reading revolution' of the late eighteenth century saw an explosion of recreational literature and an expansion of the periodical press, causing traditionalists, such as the English Romantic poet William Wordsworth (1770–1850), to express concern about the spread of what they regarded as rapid and superficial reading. A cynic might suggest that Wordsworth was disgruntled because his own poetry was not selling well, but educators and other members of the literary elite echoed his complaint that the classics were being neglected as large numbers of readers turned to popular literature, particularly sentimental novels.

Packages of books arrive from all over Europe at a shop called 'A l'Égide de Minerve' (Under the Aegis of Minerva, named after the Roman goddess of wisdom) in this scene from 1780 by the Belgian painter Léonard Defrance. A group of scholars gather to exchange greetings and ideas. Defrance was a supporter of the Enlightenment and in fact had little sympathy for the clerics represented in the foreground.

In the nineteenth century, the Western world achieved almost universal literacy, even though school attendance was very low until the last decades of the century. Britain and France learned to read before, and not after, universal primary schooling became available and compulsory. Generalized literacy always had plenty of opponents. Conservative elites feared that educated peasants would acquire dangerous ideas, and might have the means and desire to abandon their life of back-breaking work in the countryside to find alternative employment in the city. In the eighteenth century, some American colonies banned teaching writing to black slaves. After the American Revolution, the southern states banned teaching slaves to read as well. Making reading and writing more accessible might lead to ideological challenges and possibly rebellion. Upheavals such as the English Civil War of the 1640s and the French Revolution of 1789 reinforced the upper-class fear of literacy. Members of the owning class preferred employees who neither asked questions nor developed unsuitable ambitions for social promotion. Only late in the nineteenth century did some more enlightened factory-owners begin to see literacy as an advantage in maintaining order and good morality, a means of instilling ennobling and edifying thoughts in the workforce.

The industrialization of book production in the nineteenth century constituted another revolution of the book. A series of technological changes transformed printing and paper manufacture, and the railways created new opportunities for distribution and marketing on a national and international scale. Metal presses, steam presses and paper industrially manufactured from vegetable matter instead of old cloth all assisted a surge in book production, and helped to make books cheaper than ever before. It was in the nineteenth century, too, that the book trades as a whole developed a modern and now familiar business model. From the second half of the century onwards, a workable system emerged in the West that at last provided due rewards for authors, booksellers, printers and publishers. This system relied for the first time on the payment of royalties – a percentage of the profit based on the number of copies sold – to authors, and on international copyright protection for all the specialized professions involved in the business of creating intellectual property.

The electronic revolution, lastly, is the biggest change since the codex. It has altered the physical form of the book, by simply removing completely its traditional supporting material: paper. Revolutions in electronic communications have produced similar responses and aroused similar fears to those that greeted the invention of printing over 500 years ago. On the one hand, the internet, just like the printing press, offers boundless scope for the production and dissemination of knowledge, but, like the printing press, it can also transmit lies and nonsense more effectively. The fifteenth-century Roman Catholic Church, just like some sovereign governments today, saw its control over the dissemination of knowledge weakening. Viewed in the wider context of the 'living history' of books, many contemporary concerns surrounding the internet and the rise of electronic books echo the panicked, naïve rhetoric that circulated when printing first appeared.

Printing presses and equipment from the Plantin–Moretus workshop, the publishing house founded in 1555 by Christopher Plantin, and run by his son-in-law Jan Moretus and descendants from 1589 onwards. The building in Antwerp is now a museum of printing history. In the foreground is a copy of 'Le Bonheur de ce Monde' (The Happiness of this World), a poem by Christopher Plantin.

In the field of information technology, the recent rate of change seems astonishingly rapid. If we imagine the entire history of textual communication as a calendar year, with the beginnings of writing in Sumer on 1 January, the codex was invented in September, Gutenberg produced his moveable type in late November, and the internet, the most fundamental change of all, was invented around noon on 31 December, and electronic books around sunset. Ours is not the first 'information society' on earth, and it surely will not be the last.

The Workers of the Book

The story of the book is not a story about big-name authors. Book production has always depended on its social, political, economic and cultural contexts. The history of literary production cannot be reduced to a tale of famous novelists, Booker or Goncourt Prize winners or, for example, the commemorative plaques to great Australian writers embedded in the walkway that I take to get to the Sydney Opera House. The history of books also embraces niche-interest and low-status genres such as science fiction, Japanese graphic novels and romance novelettes. So there is no need in this book to pay exaggerated respect to literary reputations. As Bertolt Brecht's poem 'Questions from a Worker Who Reads' (1935) asks: 'Where, the evening that the Wall of China was

finished/ Did the masons go?' In surveying the great literature of the world, we should sometimes ask a similar question: who actually *made* the books?

Authors do not write books; they write texts. Texts are shaped, transformed and interpreted by editors, designers and illustrators. A choice of format, paper and price has to be made by the publisher. The paper itself must be manufactured. The texts must be set in type, printed and bound; in earlier eras they had to be hand-copied laboriously by scribes. Publicity and advertising put commercial strategies into action by targeting particular consumer markets. And warehousing and distribution systems hold stock and send it out to booksellers. The author, whose individual creative genius was put on a pedestal by the Romantic movement, is in reality only one element in a complicated chain of production.

Readers, too, are an essential element in the process, perhaps the most important of all, and reading, too, has its history. Many readers, especially in the past, when books were rare and costly, respected them as vital sources of illumination or intellectual liberation; others turned to literature purely for escape and recreation. Modern readers in wealthy countries often treat books as consumer products, easily discarded and replaced in a frantic search for something new. We sometimes read as though we have just taken a crash course in speed reading, and the art of slow reading, like the art of 'slow food', is disappearing.

Defining the book itself is a risky operation. I prefer to be inclusive rather than exclusive, and so I offer a very loose definition. The book, for example, does not simply exist as a bound text of sheets of printed paper – the traditional codex with which we are most familiar today. Such a definition forgets two millennia of books before print, and the various forms that textual communication took before the codex was invented.

Rows of shelves in the distribution warehouse of online retailer Amazon.com, in Fernley, Nevada. Although e-book sales are rising fast, Amazon reported in 2010 that sales of physical books were also increasing.

A traditional definition based only on the codex would also exclude hypertext and the virtual book, which have done away with the book's conventional material support. I prefer to embrace all these forms, from cuneiform script to the printed codex to the digitized electronic book, and to trace the history of the book as far back as the invention of writing systems themselves. The term 'book', then, is a kind of shorthand that stands for many forms of written textual communication adopted in past societies, using a wide variety of materials.

The main geographical focus of what follows lies in Europe and North America, and the chronological rhythm of my chapters is dictated by events in the Western world. At the same time, the West cannot claim rights of seniority in the history of books and of writing. The story must go back at least to Mesopotamian writing systems, and must recognize the origins of printing not only in Europe but also in China and Korea. Book production today is, of course, not confined to the West, as the substantial literary production of Japan, South America and the Middle East illustrates. The West was important, however, because the printing press was born there, and because universal literacy was achieved there first, along with all the cultural and political repercussions that widespread literacy entailed. The electronic revolution, too, originated in the West, even if its ramifications are global. I look, therefore, towards broad horizons, while concentrating on individual case studies to illuminate the panorama. Aldus Manutius and Christopher Plantin, for example, stand for new developments in Renaissance printing and publishing, while Walter Scott stands for the rise of mass fiction. Throughout this book, local stories define global trends.

A Manipuri priest reads prayers from an ancient religious book in the Sri Govindaji temple in Imphal, India, which is dedicated to Krishna.

1 ANCIENT AND MEDIEVAL WORLDS

In the ancient world, reading and writing were confined to a small bureaucratic and clerical elite. In ancient Egypt, for example, probably only 1 per cent of the population could write, and this limited group consisted of the pharaoh, his administrative cadres, the army leaders, perhaps some of their wives, and the priests. Ancient societies wrote in pictures or symbols, on bark, palm or banana leaves, wood, clay, papyrus, tortoise shells, bamboo or silk. Meanwhile the mass of the population lived on the margins of literacy.

Ancient societies made some crucial advances: China invented paper and the Greeks developed a highly influential alphabet (although they were not the first to invent alphabetical script). Of all ancient societies, Rome was perhaps the one that enjoyed the most widespread literacy. Only through written communication could its legal system and its military power be administered and enforced, from Britain to North Africa and from Spain to the Danube.

The slow decline of Rome and the onset of the 'barbarian' invasions produced the collapse of this literate world from about the sixth century CE. Literacy declined and scholarship was under siege. When the Viking scourge was unleashed on the coasts of northern Europe in the eighth and ninth centuries, the raiders targeted cultural centres such as the monasteries, which stored not only books but also precious objects that the invaders looted. But during these so-called 'Dark Ages', two momentous and creative developments occurred: the codex was increasingly preferred to the scroll, and silent reading gradually superseded reading aloud.

A detail of a Gallo-Roman relief showing a boy with a scroll receiving a lesson from a Greek teacher. Dating from the third or second century BCE, it forms part of a grave pillar in Neumagen an der Mosel (ancient Gaul, now Germany).

Mesopotamia

The ancient peoples of our planet left us their earliest written traces on rocks and cave walls. As recently as 1940, pictorial representations of deer and bison were discovered in the caves of Lascaux in south-west France, dating from about 15,000 BCE. In the Cueva de las Monedas in Spain, there are representations of reindeer dating from the Ice Age. The ochre rock paintings of Australian Aborigines in Kakadu may predate these European examples by thousands or even tens of thousands of years. These are examples of writing as pictorial images. Writing as a completely coded system of record emerged much later, around the start of the fourth millennium BCE, in the urban temple bureaucracies of what is now southern Iraq.

This form of writing, known as cuneiform, was born in Sumer. Here accountants recorded assets with a pointed stylus in signs and numbers on clay tablets about the size of a credit card. The action of pressing a wedge into soft clay gave this writing system its modern name (in Latin, *cuneus* means a wedge). After inscription, the tablets were simply left in the sun to dry.

Later on, Mesopotamian writing came to be used for other purposes: to record legal contracts, to make inscriptions to the gods and to compose narratives. By the second millennium BCE scribal schools existed to teach the esoteric art of writing – in the 1950s, archaeologists discovered one in Nippur, close to the river Euphrates. Tablets were also used to write down Sumerian literature, as well as myths, hymns to the gods and even

A Sumerian cuneiform tablet, dating from *c.* 2100 BCE, used for keeping temple accounts.

The so-called 'flood tablet' from the epic of *Gilgamesh*, from Nineveh in northern Iraq, dates from the seventh century BCE. One of twelve tablets, it tells in the Akkadian language how the hero Utnapishtim built a boat to survive the great flood which the gods had warned him was imminent.

jokes. Between the middle of the nineteenth and the start of the twentieth centuries, 25,000 tablets were found at Nineveh, made up of epic literature and interpretations of omens (horoscopy) in the Akkadian language. These tablets were from the scholarly library of King Ashurbanipal of Nineveh (668–*c*. 630 BCE), which also yielded the Assyrian version of the epic of *Gilgamesh*. The story of *Gilgamesh* tells of a mythical king of the Sumerian city of Uruk and his exploits in search of immortality. It includes a flood episode reminiscent of the biblical deluge.

In Mesopotamia, as in many other ancient societies, literacy was restricted to a handful of professionals. The cuneiform tablets used to record taxation and legal matters were the sole provenance of bureaucrats. Priests claimed a monopoly on interpreting sacred books, just as they alone could 'read' the messages revealed in the entrails of sacrificial animals. Knowledge of writing made them privileged intermediaries between earthly existence and the life beyond.

In this Assyrian relief dating from the eighth or seventh century BCE, two scribes (in the centre) record the booty piled up after a successful military campaign. Such narrative decorations served to glorify the achievements of the king.

Ancient China

The oldest known Chinese script dates from around 1400 BCE. Excavations at the Xiaotun site on the Huan river in the north of Henan province have uncovered over 50,000 inscriptions on tortoise shells, incorporating some 4,500 different characters. (Chinese script may in fact be thousands of years older than this: comparable symbols unearthed at Jiahu in Henan in 2003 date from as early as 6600 BCE, but experts are divided as to whether they qualify as writing.) This early Chinese writing had a divinatory purpose. Magicians read the lines that appeared in fire-cracked tortoise shells or ox scapulae to receive answers to their clients' questions, often etching the 'answers' into the surface with a knife for greater clarity. The questions were usually inscribed from the top downwards, starting from the right – still the traditional orientation for Chinese script. This technique enabled the shaman to contact a supernatural universe through his mastery of reading and writing.

China's first recognizable books, in use by the sixth century BCE, were *jiance* or *jiandu* – rolls of thin bamboo or wooden strips inscribed with indelible ink and fastened by cord. A bamboo stem was stripped of its outer skin and cut into selected lengths of 20–70 centimetres (8–28 inches). These were split lengthways into centimetre-wide strips, then dried over a fire to form individual tablets, each holding a single vertical column of characters. The strips were bound together with hemp, silk or leather to form books that could be rolled up into bundles. Vulnerable to decay and fading ink, early surviving examples of *jiance* are scarce, but the technology continued to be used long after paper was invented. Early Chinese books were used mainly for institutional purposes by civil or military officials, but from Confucius onwards (551–479 BCE), books became important instruments of learning, transmitting treatises on philosophy, medicine, astronomy and cartography.

Silk was extensively used as a surface for writing, especially during the Warring States period (475–221 BCE). The fabric was light, it survived the damp climate of the Yangtze region, absorbed ink well, and provided a white background for the text. However, it was far more expensive than bamboo – sometimes a rough copy was made on bamboo before important texts and illustrated books were inscribed on silk.

Chinese tradition attributes the invention of paper to a eunuch of the imperial court called Cai Lun in 105 CE. He used new ingredients – old rags, hemp, tree bark and fishing nets – to develop a method of paper-making fundamentally similar to that still used today. Fibres were soaked in water until the individual filaments separated, then lifted out on a fine mesh screen to form a thin layer of matted fibre that could be dried and bleached. Paper took hundreds of years to replace bamboo and silk, but by the end of the second century CE the imperial court was already using it in significant amounts.

A turtle plastron from Anyang in Henan province, China, dating from the Shang dynasty in the twelfth century BCE. The protective shell of the turtle's underbelly was subjected to heat, producing significant cracks in the process. The cracks could then be interpreted for predictions about the rain, the harvest or the likely outcome of a military expedition. The 'answers' were often etched into the surface with a knife.

Bamboo strips containing a partial transcription of the *Laozi*, the fundamental text of Taoism, from the Warring States period. Three bundles of such strips were found in 1993 in tomb no.1 at Guodian, near Jingmen City in Hubei province, China.

The technology did not spread outside China until around 610 CE, reaching Europe via Spain only in the twelfth century.

Paper was pivotal in the spread of Confucianism, which was adopted as a state doctrine by the Han dynasty in the second century BCE. Confucian writings were initially transmitted by the Han rulers to their subjects via large carved stone slabs. The earliest slabs still legible date from 175 CE, when the reigning emperor ordered stone copies of the *Five Classics* and the *Analects of Confucius*. This 'library' took eight years to complete and covered nearly fifty stones, each 1.75 metres (5 feet 8 inches) high, with over 200,000 characters in all. With the advent of paper, these stone-slab 'books' permitted a primitive form of printing: by placing a sheet of paper on the stone and rubbing graphite over the upper side, a scholar could quickly create a copy of the text with the indented characters picked out in white on a black background.

The Chinese invented woodblock, or xylographic, printing some time before the mid-eighth century. Woodblock printing did not need the hard pressure of a printing press to make an imprint: instead, the printer rubbed the back of the page as it lay on an inked carved block. Only one side of the paper could be used in this method, but the equipment could be carried and operated by a single man, producing thousands of pages a day. The need to reproduce large numbers of Buddhist texts and images promoted the early spread of xylography; calendars, divinatory manuals and dictionaries were also in demand. The earliest Chinese printed book yet found is the *Diamond Sutra* of 868 CE from Dunhuang, a walled-in treasure trove of paper documents first excavated in the early 1900s, but it was not until the tenth century that printing became widespread. Emperor Ming Tsung (r. 926–933 CE) authorized the reproduction of the Confucian *Classics* from xylographs, after which the method rapidly became the chief means of book production in China.

Chinese printers first created moveable type around 1100 CE, but this development did not revolutionize printing to the same extent as Gutenberg's independent reinvention of the technology in Europe 400 years later. Unlike European languages, which use a small number of letters, written Chinese required thousands of unique characters, making individually cut woodblocks far more efficient than enormous sets of reusable type. Moreover, in contrast with the decline of the scribal arts in the West in the centuries following Gutenberg, Chinese calligraphy retained its prestige after the advent of printing. Calligraphy was a prized social art, and the belief persisted that the best way to absorb the contents of a book was to copy it by hand. Nonetheless, by the end of the fifteenth century China had produced more books than the rest of the world put together.

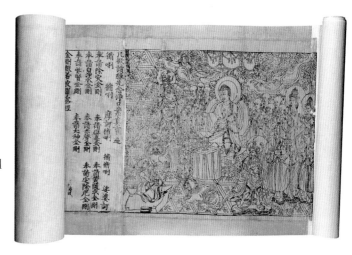

This Diamond Sutra is the earliest dated printed book. The sutra contains a dialogue with the Buddha, and this woodblock copy from the British Library dates from 868 CE, almost 600 years before Gutenberg invented his printing method. It forms part of a scroll nearly 5 metres (16 feet) long.

Papyrus, Parchment, Paper

Papyrus, the earliest form of paper, was used to make books in Egypt, Greece and Rome. Thucydides (*c.* 460–400 BCE), Plato (*c.* 428–*c.* 347 BCE) and Cicero (106–43 BCE) all wrote on papyrus. Egypt exported papyrus all over the Mediterranean world.

Egypt monopolized production and jealously guarded the secrets of manufacturing papyrus from reeds growing in the marshes of the Nile Delta. Strips were carefully peeled away from the stem of the reed, and laid out in one layer. Next a second layer was put on top of them at right angles to the first layer. Then the papyrus sheet was pressed – the fluid from the plant held the layers together. Finished sheets were polished with pumice stone or shells. Since the papyrus sheet consisted of two superimposed layers, a different grain ran across each side, hence the recto (where the grain ran horizontally) and verso (where the grain ran vertically). Usually, however, papyrus carried writing only on the smooth side. Sheets could be cut to the required size and, if necessary, glued together to make a longer roll. In the Pharaonic period, rolls were usually no longer than 6 metres (20 feet), although much longer ones have been found in tombs. A wooden stick would be attached to the last sheet. This was the navel (*umbilicus* in Latin), which made the book easier to handle.

From the first century CE onwards, parchment began to compete with papyrus. This new technology was initially called *charta pergamena* ('Pergamon paper') in Latin, from Pergamum in modern Turkey, where it reputedly originated. Parchment offered several

This Egyptian papyrus is from the Book of the Dead of Hunefer, *c.* 1375 BCE, which was placed in the burial chamber of the deceased. The upper left panel, from right to left, shows the white tomb, an oversize stele, the mummy of Hunefer supported by a priest wearing the jackal mask of the god Anubis, his mourning family and several white-sashed priests. The lower panel shows a calf about to be sacrificed.

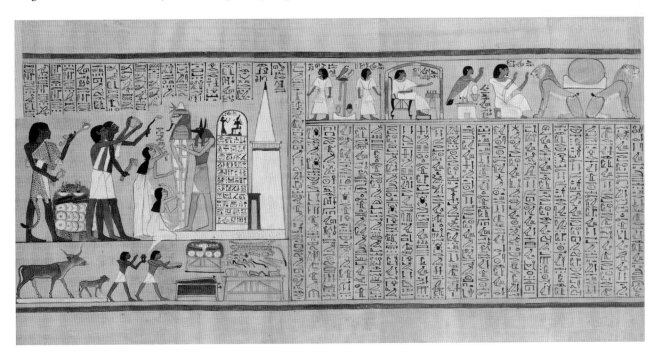

advantages over papyrus. Papyrus tended to decompose rapidly in humid conditions, which made it unsuitable for use in Europe's damper regions. Parchment, on the other hand, which derived from animal skins, was more durable, and could withstand being folded and stitched to other sheets. It could be scraped clean and reused (the term 'palimpsest' originally described a page that had been recycled in this fashion). Parchment also brought economic benefits for the Romans: unlike papyrus, it did not have to be imported from Egypt. But parchment required careful preparation. Animal hide had to be dried, scraped clean, smoothed with pumice stone and then polished. Today we cut down forests to produce newsprint; in the first centuries CE, writing on parchment required the slaughter of livestock. Cattle, sheep, goats, rabbits and sometimes even squirrels became parchment. Calfskin (vellum) was considered the best of all. The twelfth-century Winchester Bible, for example, consumed 250 calfskins, but over 2,000 hides were first collected before those with blemishes were rejected. This level of consumption was only possible in a society where writing was not a widespread practice. Parchment production was expensive, and so it was prudent to make rough copies on wax tablets before entrusting the final version to a scribe. In the late Roman and early medieval periods, official documents and deluxe manuscripts were written in gold and silver ink on parchment that had been dyed or painted with costly purple pigments as an expression of imperial power and wealth.

This richly coloured parchment is from the Codex Aureus, an illuminated gospel book produced in the eleventh century at the Benedictine Abbey of Echternach (today in Luxembourg). The scene depicts the parable of the vineyard.

Paper originated in China, where it came into widespread use in the late second century CE. Chinese paper was very thin and usually only one side could be used for writing. The Arabs learned the technique of paper-making from Chinese contacts in the eighth century, and it was from the Arab world, via Islamic Spain, that paper was introduced to Europe in the twelfth century.

Ancient Greece

The introduction of alphabetic script has been heralded as a decisive advance that made reading and writing skills more accessible. The Greek alphabet, which developed in the sixth and fifth centuries BCE, was different from earlier sign systems because it was purely phonetic; that is to say, unlike Chinese ideograms, the alphabet represented the sounds of the human voice. In finding a way to transcribe vowels, consonants and syllables, the Greeks produced a sign system that would eventually break down clerical monopolies on writing. A Chinese scholar could devote a whole lifetime to mastering thousands of characters; in comparison, the Greek alphabet could be learned in a few days.

Although the Greeks are often credited with this innovation, their phonetic alphabet was not unique. They borrowed, for example, from the Phoenician alphabet which used symbols to represent sounds. The Semitic languages Hebrew and Aramaic also had their own alphabets. In these other scripts, the alphabet consisted only of consonants, but the Greeks added vowels. Although this made reading easier, literacy in ancient Greece was not widespread. The use of writing grew in Athens from about the fifth century BCE, but other city-states, such as Sparta, lagged behind. Even in Athens, peasants, slaves and most women were illiterate, and books were rare objects. The tragedian Euripides possessed a library of several papyrus scrolls, but this was quite exceptional.

A wax writing tablet from Greece dating from the second century CE, used for student exercises. Two neat lines of writing at the top (possibly from the poet Menander) were copied twice by the student below. Holes were drilled through the wax to hold several tablets together.

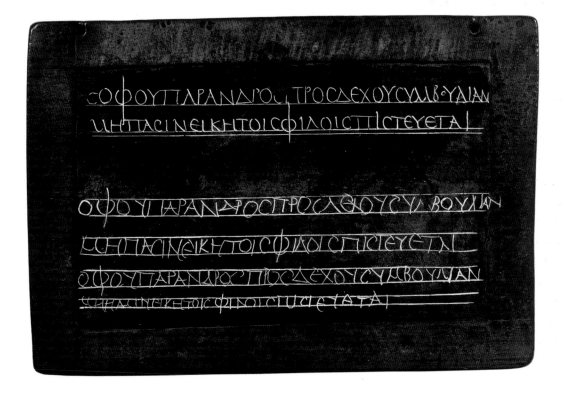

Unlike Semitic languages, which were written from right to left, Greek was written and read from left to right. Occasionally, however, the writer would start the next line where the previous line finished, so that the lines would read alternately left to right, then right to left, and so on. This 'boustrophedon' writing, which was said to imitate the path of the ox-drawn plough, remained in use until the sixth century. The Greeks, like the Romans, wrote in *scriptio continua*: that is to say, they produced seamless texts, with no space between words and no interruptions for new paragraphs. The script was completely unpunctuated and, at the end of a line, words just ran over into the next line. Such completely unbroken script is very hard to read; the only way to comprehend it is to speak it aloud. When it becomes oral speech, the natural breaks appear and the text acquires meaning. This is how the ancient Greeks envisaged reading; it was an oral performance, as exemplified by the private poetry recital (the symposium). The author's

The Constitution of Athens, probably written by Aristotle or one of his pupils *c*. 350 BCE, and discovered at Oxyrhynchus in Egypt in 1890.

role resembled that of a musical composer. His job was not complete until someone transferred his text into sound by reciting it aloud.

Homer's *Iliad*, which emerged around 700 BCE, was based on a long tradition of oral composition by various authors. 'Homer' himself was probably a number of different poets whose identities are largely unknown. Some of the work may have been recited from memory, other portions improvised in the course of performance. Far from being the creation of a single genius, the *Iliad* inherited the creative efforts of generations, and that heritage was renewed and transformed by a series of individual poets. 'Homer' was the product of a society in which oral communication still predominated.

There was little paper in ancient Greece, and all sorts of materials were appropriated for textual communication, including pieces of leather or snakeskin. Athenians scribbled notes on shards of pottery – this was their scrap paper. Legal documents played an increasingly important role in Athenian life, but libraries and archives were slow to develop. The city archive at the Metröon in Athens, established in 405 BCE, stored documents in sealed jars and was extraordinarily difficult to consult by modern standards. In Paros, contracts were deposited in the temple for security and as an additional safety precaution a public curse was put on anybody tampering with them. Outside Athens, custom and tradition rather than written record governed legal processes. Greeks still relied extensively on individual memory.

Above: Greek amphora from 490–480 BCE, attributed to the Kleophrades painter of Athens, showing a bearded poet holding a staff and mounted on a plinth with text cascading from his mouth.

Left: Pottery shards (*ostraka*) from the Athenian agora, inscribed with a stylus, dating from 487–416 BCE. Three bear the name of politician and general Themistocles, who was banished from the city.

The Great Library of Alexandria

Ptolemy II Philadelphus is shown conversing with scholars in the library of Alexandria in this 1813 work by the Italian neo-classicist painter Vincenzo Camuccini (1771–1844). Camuccini was probably inviting parallels with Napoleon, portraying him as a patron of the arts.

The most celebrated library of the ancient world was established in Alexandria, Egypt, in the first half of the third century BCE, during the reigns of Ptolemy I Soter and Ptolemy II Philadelphus, kings of Egypt (322–246 BCE). The library was part of a museum, which included a garden, a common dining room, a reading room, lecture theatres and meeting rooms, creating a model for the modern university campus.

Attempts were made to gather together all the knowledge of the known world. Messengers were sent to buy items at the book fairs of Rhodes and Athens. International scholars came on funded visits. According to Galen, all ships visiting Alexandria were obliged to surrender their books for immediate copying – the owners received a copy, but the pharaohs kept the originals in their museum. The Alexandrian library collection included the best available texts of Greek authors and also of non-Greek works, such as the Hebrew Old Testament. In this way, the museum asserted the power of the Ptolemaic kings over both the Greek and non-Hellenic worlds.

At its height, the library of Alexandria was said to possess nearly half a million scrolls. In the mid-third century BCE, the poet Callimachus was employed there, and created the first ever alphabetically arranged library catalogue. Ptolemy II Philadelphus even set up an offshoot library, the Serapeum, which was more of a public library, whereas the main library was designed for scholars.

Collecting Greek books in imitation of Alexandria became a sign of cultural status, and the library at Pergamum was established in the second half of the third century BCE in direct competition with Alexandria. Greek scholarship enjoyed enormous prestige. The study of Homer, for example, was considered essential for an educated man. Many papyrus fragments of Homer were found in Egypt. Euripides (480–*c.* 406 BCE) and Demosthenes (384–322 BCE) were also part of the curriculum in Hellenized Mediterranean cities such as Oxyrhynchus, Ephesus, Pergamum and Corinth.

According to a spurious legend, the library of Alexandria burned down in 48 BCE when Julius Caesar set fire to the Egyptian navy, and the flames accidentally spread to the onshore port installations. Although Caesar's fire may have destroyed a book depot, the library was not situated near the port. In fact, Greek scholars reported working in the library twenty years later. It was probably destroyed when Alexandria was captured by the Roman emperor Aurelianus in 273 CE. In 2002 the Bibliotheca Alexandrina, a major library and museum complex supported by Alexandria University, UNESCO and the Egyptian government, was established close to the site of the ancient library, with the aim of re-establishing Alexandria as one of the great intellectual and cultural centres of the twenty-first century.

Above: A papyrus fragment with lines from Homer's *Odyssey*, from the early Hellenistic period, *c.* 285–50 BCE, found in Egypt. Papyrus was usually inscribed with a sharpened reed using black ink. The library of Alexandria made a point of collecting Homeric texts.

Left: In the new Bibliotheca Alexandrina, the main reading room is located beneath a 32-metre (104 foot) glass-panelled roof which is tilted out towards the sea like a sundial and measures 160 metres (524 feet) in diameter. The walls are made of grey Aswan granite and engraved with characters from 120 different scripts.

Ancient Rome

Imperial Rome was saturated with writing. The city was covered with public inscriptions: on altars at street crossings, on sarcophagi, on public monuments and on boundary markers. The everyday administration of the far-flung empire required a growing class of legal, military and bureaucratic personnel, who produced a constant flow of documentation. At the height of the empire, rudimentary literacy was common even among the plebeian class. The graffiti that survive at Ostia, Pompeii and Herculaneum suggest the presence of a large class of soldiers and artisans who had elementary but imperfect writing skills (as well as a taste for obscenity, judging by the lewd references to sexual acts in the Ostia examples).

Red election graffiti on the Street of Abundance in Pompeii.

The first great libraries in Rome consisted of treasures taken in war. Aemilius Paulus (*c.* 229–160 BCE), for example, seized the books of the Macedonian king Perseus and brought them to Rome. No public libraries were established in the city until the time of Julius Caesar (100–44 BCE) and his successor Augustus (63 BCE–14 CE), who founded the library of Apollo on the Palatine hill, but prominent Roman figures maintained private collections of books. Cicero (106–43 BCE) had collections of both Greek and Latin books in Rome as well as in his two country villas. Greek scholarship was highly respected by this bilingual Roman elite: in the first century BCE, Lucullus (118–57 BCE) was praised by the historian and philosopher Plutarch for opening his own library to Greek scholars, and for providing galleries and small side rooms where they could take a break from work. Books were part of a leisured aristocratic world – they were not familiar objects to the Roman masses.

Despite their growing fondness for books, aristocratic Romans continued to maintain the prestige of traditional oral literary culture. The most common form was reading aloud from papyrus scrolls written in *scriptio continua*. Rich patrons would employ a lector or possibly keep a slave to read aloud in their households. In the first century, epic poems were commonly recited before invited audiences; in this way the less educated could 'hear' their books. Virgil (70–19 BCE) was praised for the performance of his work. But oral performance could go too far – cultivating the vulgar public could demean the prestige of an epic work, according to the poet Horace (65–8 BCE). Pleasing and titillating the crowd was sometimes regarded as effeminate in Rome's macho culture.

In the first few centuries CE, the Roman reading public widened. Ovid (43 BCE–*c.* 18 CE), for example, wrote not just for a circle of intimate friends but for an anonymous audience that included women. Astrological predictions, and erotic, sentimental and escapist literature all appealed to the uneducated reader. In the first century CE, the philosopher Seneca (3 BCE–65 CE) deplored the way the uncultured rich decorated their houses with books they never studied.

By the third century, the great Roman libraries of the past had ceased to exist. The decline of the Roman empire and the onslaught of the 'barbarian' invasions led to a contraction of written culture. Literacy, and the urban infrastructure that supported and demanded written communication, collapsed. This precipitated the irreversible decline of many Roman scholastic institutions, with the exception of those maintained by the Christian Church.

A fresco at Pompeii depicting a woman browsing through a scroll.

Japanese Concertina Books and *The Tale of Genji*

Concertina books first reached Japan from China in the Heian period (794–1191 CE), when they were known as *orihon*. They were typically made of several sheets of paper pasted together in a long strip and then folded alternately one way and then the other in concertina-style. They might be unbound or secured by a thread passed along the edge and finished with a panel cover, a wooden board or thick protective paper. Often a fine glossy paper derived from mulberry fibres was used (*torinokogami*).

Concertina-style binding was perhaps inspired by the palm-leaf books of Buddhist texts carried on the trade routes from India to China. They were more easily transportable than scrolls, and could be progressively folded and unfolded by the reader. The traditional Japanese *orihon* carried images and text on one side only, and recorded Buddhist scriptures. Some concertina albums of painting and calligraphy, however, were pasted together so that both sides could be written on. The format continued to be used in modern times for Buddhist prayer books, calendars and folding maps.

From the twelfth century onwards, one of the most popular books to appear in concertina format was *The Tale of Genji*, a long prose romance authored by Murasaki Shikibu (*c.* 973–*c.* 1031 CE), a lady of the court. Its fifty-four chapters tell the story of the career and amorous adventures of Prince Hikaru Genji, the son of an emperor and a

The earliest written scroll of *The Tale of Genji,* a long Japanese courtly romance which is claimed to be the first novel in the world.

concubine, who, because of his mother's low birth, is denied any right of succession to the throne. In the sexual politics of court life, Genji's women play a passive role, observing the main action discreetly from behind screens and curtains. The characters' emotional moods are reflected in the passing of the seasons and other natural phenomena. The story has Buddhist overtones: desire always leads to penance and retribution. *Genji* was a court favourite, read aloud to the emperor, and illustrated in picture scrolls and concertina books richly decorated with gold and silver leaf. *Genji* images would later appear on elegant fans, furniture and folding screens. In 1650, Harumasa Yamamoto's edition illustrated the story with 227 woodcuts. Today, *The Tale of Genji* can be read in *manga* (Japanese comic book) format, which continues a thousand-year-old tradition of combining text and image in what may be the world's earliest novel.

Two seventeenth-century illustrations of *The Tale of Genji*. On the left, a scene by Kyoto artist Yamamoto Shunsho (1610–82); on the right, a panel by Sumiyoshi Hiromichi, adopting a high-angle view distinctive of the school to which he belonged.

Ancient Buddhist Texts

The Buddha is thought to have achieved *nirvana* (enlightenment) at some time in the fifth or sixth centuries BCE. After his death, his teachings (the Dharma) survived for generations through oral transmission. Buddhist dogma was not given written form until the first century BCE.

At the beginning of the Common Era, a canon of essential Buddhist texts, known as the Tripitaka, started to emerge. The canon was very flexible, given that Buddhism was divided into different sects scattered all over Asia, each developing its own tradition.

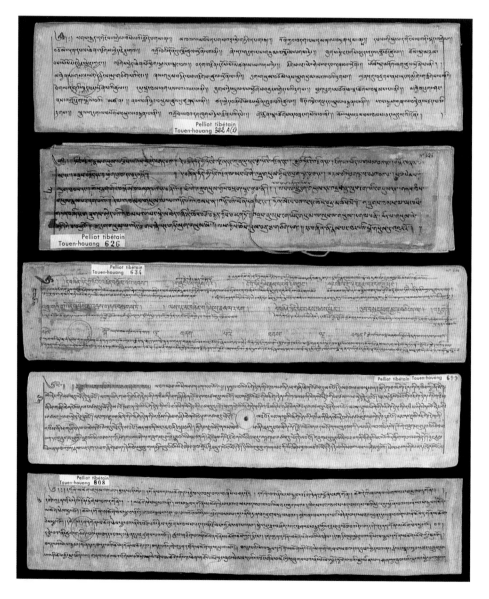

Palm-leaf sutras from Tibet carried Buddhist texts from India to China. These are from a cache of documents found by French sinologist Paul Pelliot in a sealed cave at Dunhuang, China, on the ancient Silk Road, in 1908.

Buddhist texts were produced in a variety of languages and a multitude of scripts, and monks journeyed enormous distances across Asia with them. In Sri Lanka they were composed in Pali or Sinhala, in India in Sanskrit or Tamil. Buddhist scriptures were also written in Burmese, Khmer, Thai, Chinese, Tibetan and Uighur. The Rhinoceros Sutra, for example, which teaches the virtues of solitude, exists in fragmentary form in Pali, Sanskrit and Gandharan (an ancient language of the kingdom of Gandhara, which was located in modern-day Pakistan and Afghanistan).

Even after textual production got under way, Buddhists still valued the art of memorizing and reciting the sutras, which were doctrinal teachings in aphoristic or narrative format. Buddhist texts were sacred and venerated objects. The act of copying them could bring a scribe closer to perfection and earn him merit. Mongolian and Chinese Buddhist scribes used a writing brush, and developed coloured ink illustrations using cinnabar, gold, silver and a number of other precious substances such as turquoise, lapis lazuli and mother-of-pearl. In the eighteenth century, Mongolians even used scented ink to enhance the prestige of the text.

The library at Haeinsa Temple in Korea houses the Tripitaka Koreana, a collection from the thirteenth century consisting of over 80,000 wood blocks engraved with Buddhist scriptures.

Buddhist scribes usually wrote on palm leaves, which were dried and cut into strips of roughly equal size. They would then be inscribed with a metal stylus and blackened with ink. When it dried, the excess ink was wiped away, leaving the text in black. Holes were then punched in the leaves so that they could be drawn together with string, and they were secured between wooden boards. In regions where the palm did not normally grow, birch bark was commonly used. Writing took many different forms: on scrolls or bound leaves, and sometimes on cloth, silk or metal plates. After the seventh century, Chinese woodblock printing was used, for example, in Tibet, but hand-copying and illustrating the Sutras was still a high-prestige occupation.

Palm-leaf manuscripts were fragile: in Sri Lanka, for instance, they rotted in the humid climate or were eaten by rats and insects. Because they had to be recopied constantly, Buddhist texts were not immutable scriptures; instead they were continually revived, with variations creeping in at every recopying. In more recent times, these texts suffered destruction at the hands of Christianizing colonizers, such as the Portuguese in Sri Lanka in the sixteenth and seventeenth centuries, and appropriation by European collectors in the nineteenth century. The manuscripts have also survived periodic attacks by Communist revolutionaries in the twentieth century and the hostility of Muslim extremists in our own time.

Shelves with sacred scriptures at the Dege Sutra Printing House, Garze Tibetan Autonomous Prefecture, Sichuan province, China. Built in the seventh century, this house contains 200,000 Tibetan books in the form of wooden boards.

From Scroll to Codex

The invention of the codex was one of the most significant and enduring revolutions in the history of the book. It appeared in the first centuries of the Christian era, and gave the book the distinctive and recognizable material form that it retained for seventeen centuries to come: instead of a scroll (*volumen*) it increasingly consisted of individual pages loosely attached to each other at one side.

The scroll had ruled for hundreds of years, and it was not easily displaced. But it had several drawbacks. It could be a very clumsy medium, long and difficult to manipulate with ease. Some surviving scrolls are as long as 10 metres (33 feet). Finding specific references in a scroll was not easy, since the text was continuous and lacked page breaks, which meant that it could not be indexed. Early readers unfurled their scrolls laterally, in the opposite direction of contemporary word processors, which instead invite the reader to scroll up and down the text on screen.

A boy reads a scroll on a fragment of an Attic drinking cup *(kylix)* attributed to the Akestorides painter, *c.* 470–450 BCE. The text appears to be part of the poet Hesiod's *Catalogue of Women.*

A fifth-century mosaic from the mausoleum of Empress Galla Placidia in Ravenna. The lunette shows St Lawrence with cross and book by the grill on which he was martyred, alongside a cupboard containing the four Gospels.

The codex, in comparison, had individual pages of roughly the same size, attached to each other on one side (usually, but not invariably, on the left). It could be covered either with simple boards or with some richly decorated cloth, or even in gold and silver if it was a sacred book destined for use in a cathedral. The early Christians were among the first to adopt the codex: the earliest papyrus codices of the Bible date from the second century. Jews traditionally read the Pentateuch from a scroll; Christians may have used the codex to distinguish the physical form of their scriptures from the Torah. The codex became increasingly widespread from the fourth century onwards.

The codex was more compact and easily handled than the *volumen*. Both sides of the paper could be used, which enabled the codex to hold more text than the scroll. Many early codices were miscellaneous compilations of various texts, by different authors and

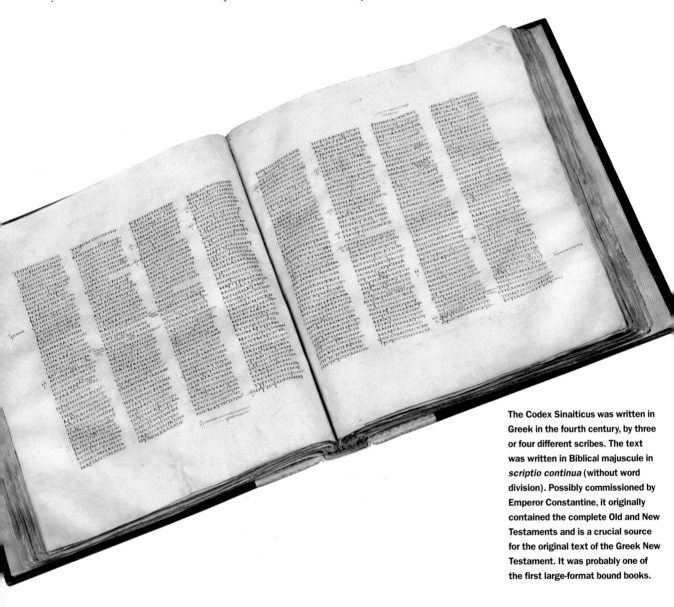

The Codex Sinaiticus was written in Greek in the fourth century, by three or four different scribes. The text was written in Biblical majuscule in *scriptio continua* (without word division). Possibly commissioned by Emperor Constantine, it originally contained the complete Old and New Testaments and is a crucial source for the original text of the Greek New Testament. It was probably one of the first large-format bound books.

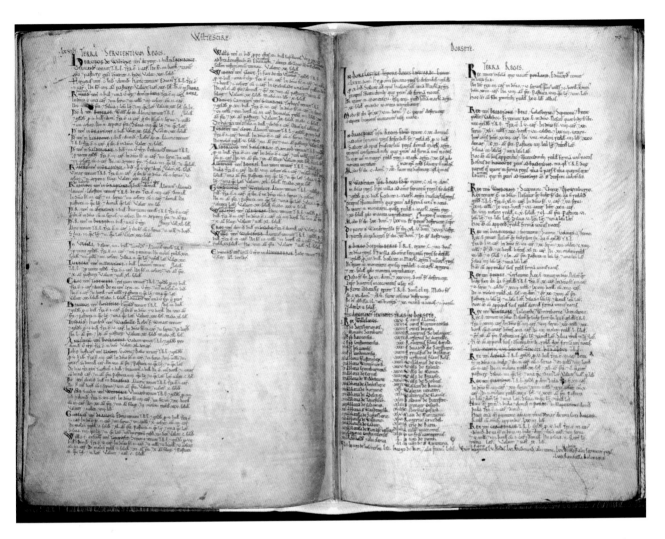

even in different languages, not necessarily on the same topic. Such codices formed miniature libraries in their own right.

The scroll had to be held in both hands, whereas the codex liberated the reader to use his or her spare hand to take notes or to hold a drink. The scholar could add page numbers and indexes to allow him to locate specific passages and quotations, which could be cross-referenced with other codices. Headings and summaries were added, and these navigational aids were essential for using the codex as a teaching instrument. Bookmarking, in other words, had become a great deal easier.

Despite the clear advantages of the codex, the scroll persisted for centuries in certain milieux. The English monarchy, for instance, still relied on scrolls to record its legislation on the so-called 'statute rolls' until well into the Middle Ages. (One exception to this custom was the Domesday survey of 1086, which was recorded in two codices, now known as the Domesday Book.) For a long time, the scroll was also used in the theatre; this is the origin of the term 'actor's role'.

The Domesday Book, completed in 1086, was the first English census. It recorded land and possessions in over 13,000 communities for taxation purposes. The name refers to the fact that it was believed to be as definitive and irreversible as the Last Judgment. This page refers to the county of Dorset. As was customary, headings and the initial letter of each paragraph were rubricated (decorated in red).

Monastic Libraries

The Rule of St Benedict of Nursia, first established in the sixth century in the monastery of Monte Cassino on the Italian peninsula, made the reading and study of Christian literature an obligation for monks. Monte Cassino was sacked by Muslim invaders in 883, but in the centuries that followed, other Benedictine monasteries – such as those at St Gall (Switzerland), Reichenau (southern Germany) and Melk (Austria) – became renowned for their manuscript collections.

In the earliest monasteries, there was no special room set aside as a library, but from the sixth century onwards libraries became an essential component of monastic life in Western Europe. The Benedictines increasingly put the books in the care of a librarian who supervised their use. In some monastic reading rooms, valuable books would be chained to the shelves, but there would be a lending section as well. The Rule of St Benedict prescribed three hours of reading per day and the reading of an entire book during Lent.

Copying, by resident or visiting monks, took place in the *scriptorium*. In the Byzantine world, in contrast, religious houses rarely maintained their own copying centres. Instead they acquired donations from wealthy benefactors. In the tenth century, the largest collection in the Byzantine world was to be found in the monasteries of Mount Athos (modern-day Greece), which accumulated over 10,000 books.

Scholars travelled from one monastery to another in search of the texts they wished to study – the books did not come to them. Travelling monks were often given money to buy books, and certain monasteries that had a reputation for intellectual activities welcomed itinerant monks who came to copy manuscripts for their own libraries. One of these was the monastery of Bobbio in Italy, founded by the Irish abbot St Columba in 614. By the ninth century, it boasted a catalogue of 666 manuscripts, including religious works, classical texts, histories and mathematical treatises.

Below: **A highly elaborate design decorates the 74th psalm in this mid-twelfth-century Latin psalter produced at Monte Cassino. The size of the design and its complex and dense interweaving of animal heads testify to the wealth and expertise of Benedictine monasteries.**

Opposite: **Valuable works are chained to their shelves in the library at Hereford Cathedral, England.**

ORE EST ET TVVS LOCVS   EFTERNACA VOCA OTS
EXPECTAT VENIĀ   NOCTE DIE QTVĀ

Monks at work in the *scriptorium* at Echternach (Luxembourg), which produced many luxury editions in the eleventh century, including a giant Bible measuring 60 × 40 cm (24 × 16 in.) for the abbey's own use.

All monasteries had their own liturgical books for daily use. They might be elaborately decorated, as they formed the working core of the monastery's collection and were objects of great community pride. These books would have included a Gradual, which contained the words and music to be sung as part of the Mass. Systems of musical notation were developed in the ninth century and became increasingly elaborate in Graduals from the eleventh century. In addition, the Antiphonal contained the words and music for the responses sung in various offices (services) throughout the day.

The Life of a Scribe

Talented scribes and manuscript illuminators worked in European monastic scriptoria between the seventh and fifteenth centuries. Scribes had to be able to copy religious works in Latin, Greek or Hebrew, whether they understood them or not, and they had to be familiar with writing technology in order to ensure their lines were straight and their letters of even size. They were expected to be competent in a range of scripts.

St Jerome, who translated the Bible into Latin (the Vulgate), is frequently depicted as a writer immersed in the scholarly life. In this manuscript, he is composing the life of St Paul at a tall lectern, in a pose typical of monastic scribes.

In much of ninth-century Europe, the Carolingian minuscule and its variations came into widespread use, especially for governmental purposes, while in northern Europe a form of Gothic handwriting remained popular. The English chancery hand was increasingly valued from the fourteenth century onwards for its clarity and legibility. Scribes usually copied three to four pages per day, but they were prone to human error, and even a good scribe could be expected to make at least one mistake per page.

During the twelfth and thirteenth centuries, copying became more of a professional activity and was increasingly performed by specialists. To meet expanding demand, the *pecia* (Latin for 'piece') system was introduced, in which different parts of the same text were assigned to hired copiers, possibly laymen, working both in and outside the monasteries. In German-speaking Europe, manuscript copying increased considerably in the century before the invention of printing.

The ingeniously decorated eighth-century Gellone Sacramentary from southern France was a liturgical book detailing the order of the Mass as spoken by the priest. Its Carolingian minuscule script marked a new advance in clarity, clearly differentiating upper-case from lower-case letters and including clear spaces between words.

An eleventh-century English manuscript illumination (Cambridge, Corpus Christi College MS 389, folio 1v) shows St Jerome at work at his desk. He sits in a high chair that allows his feet to dangle or perhaps rest on a platform; prolonged contact with the cold stone floors of a medieval monastery was not advisable. Behind Jerome a curtain has been tied up to give him more light as he works. Usually monks wrote only in daylight hours, because candles were too expensive, but even when candles were lit, the light was very poor by modern standards. His work is propped up at an angle on a lectern covered in cloth. Writing at this angle meant that the scribe did not have to hold the pen vertically: if he did so, the ink might run out of it too fast. The pages have already been lined, probably using a plumb line. In his right hand, Jerome is holding a quill pen, which has very little feathering left on it. In his left hand, he holds a knife, an all-purpose scribal tool used to keep the parchment firmly anchored to the copying surface, sharpen the quills, or scrape dried ink away from the parchment in the fashion of an eraser. Correcting errors was sometimes aided by a razor or pumice stone. In this image, Jerome is not copying a text, but composing one, as a dove representing the Holy Spirit hovers over his head, supplying him with inspiration.

The Book of Kells

Irish culture blossomed in Europe and the British Isles between the seventh and the ninth centuries, mainly because of the intense missionary activity of Irish monks. Irish monastic scriptoria developed a particular artistic style known as Insular. One of its most lavish expressions is found in the Book of Kells, a large-format volume of the Gospels, made up of 340 folios and most likely designed for use on the altar.

The Book of Kells began life on the island of Iona in the Scottish Inner Hebrides, where a monastery was founded by the Irish missionary St Columba in the early 560s. At the beginning of the ninth century, Viking raids compelled the resident monks to seek refuge at Kells in County Meath, in Ireland. The artist-monks probably began the manuscript on Iona but finished it after their migration to Kells. Producing it was a long and costly process, which may explain why some decorations have been left in outline – presumably unfinished.

The book opens with prefaces, summaries and concordances, followed by the four Gospels in Latin, written on calfskin (vellum) in Insular majuscule script. Most of the text was inscribed in iron-gall ink, made from iron salts and natural tannin, which became the writing ink most commonly used in the Middle Ages. The initial letters are richly decorated, and some letters are accentuated with small red dots or sophisticated interlaces to attract attention to significant passages. The illuminations consist of full-page compositions in which decorative motifs and curvilinear designs resemble early medieval Irish metalwork and stonework. The complex iconography also shows the influence of Byzantine, Armenian and Coptic art (from which came the red dots to outline letters), as well as Mediterranean models. The ornaments include figures of the

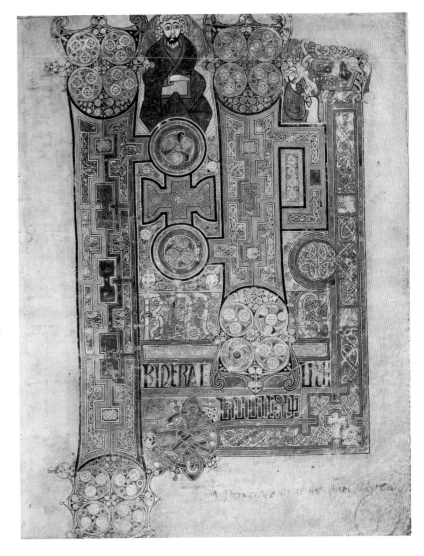

The opening of the Gospel according to John from the Book of Kells: *In principio erat verbum* ('In the beginning was the word').

The Book of Kells, showing the Virgin and child seated on the left, introducing the Gospel according to Matthew.

Virgin Mary, Christ and the Evangelists; mythical creatures such as dragons and griffins (with a lion's body and an eagle's head and wings); a variety of animals – peacocks, snakes, horses, dogs, lions and bulls, sometimes winged; and Christian emblems such as the cross and the chalice, elaborately detailed in black, red, purple and yellow. The names of the artists are lost to history.

In the seventeenth century, James Ussher, Archbishop of Armagh (1581–1656), presented the Book of Kells to Trinity College, Dublin, where it is now on permanent display in the library. Two centuries later, the pages were substantially cropped in the process of re-binding, and about thirty folios, including some major illuminated pages, were lost. In 1953 the single-volume manuscript was divided into four volumes for conservation reasons.

Books of Hours

The book of hours was a popular form of prayer book produced for the laity during the later Middle Ages and Renaissance. It indicated the prayers and devotions appropriate for specific times of day and seasons of the year. A book of hours might be commissioned by a rich patron to suit his or her taste and religious practices. Books of hours were frequently richly illuminated as a way of personalizing them. They were luxury objects, portable and usually written in Latin in Gothic script, exemplifying the way books were produced increasingly for educated lay readers, including women. Books of hours implied a private and individual engagement with the text.

One spectacular and magnificently illustrated example was *Les très riches heures du Duc de Berry*, produced in the fifteenth century for Jean, Duke of Berry (1340–1416), the brother of Charles V of France and a keen bibliophile and patron of the arts. Its illumination was begun in 1411 by the Flemish Limbourg brothers, but took years to complete and was still unfinished when the Duke died in 1416. The work was continued in the 1440s by the Flemish artist Barthélemy d'Eyck (*c.* 1420–post 1470), and

Madonna and child from the book of hours produced in Bruges at the end of the fifteenth century for Joanna I of Castile (also known as Joanna the Mad because she apparently suffered from depression). This book of 482 pages was illustrated by the Flemish artist Gerard Horenbout (*c.* 1465–1541).

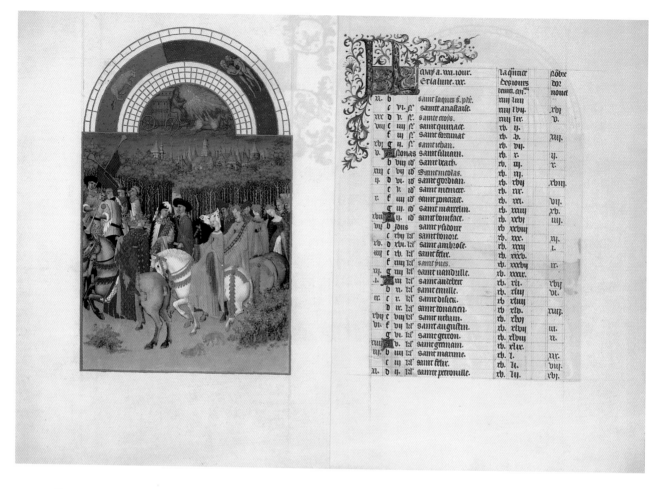

eventually carried to completion under the patronage of Charles, Duke of Savoy (1468–1490), in about 1485.

The book's miniature illustrations combine picturesque scenes of courtly life with sacred images. In the Franco-Flemish Gothic style of the period, they portray fashionable costumes, the pastimes of courtiers and the work of the peasantry at various moments of the agricultural year. The Limbourg brothers used a variety of pigments. They extracted green from Hungarian malachite, blue from grinding lapis lazuli from the Middle East, and vermilion from a combination of sulphur and mercury. The Latin text, produced in large format, was in two columns of black Gothic script with decorated initials and line-endings. The book contained a calendar of saints' days and religious festivals, extracts from the Gospels, prayers and psalms, litanies and a series of Masses for holy days.

After Charles of Savoy died, the book disappeared, but it resurfaced in the nineteenth century, having been bound in red leather by the Spinola family of Genoa during the eighteenth century. It was bought in 1856 by the Duke of Aumale, son of King Louis-Philippe of France, and it has remained in the Château de Chantilly, near Paris, ever since.

In the devotional book *Les très riches heures du Duc de Berry* the monthly calendar was juxtaposed with an image of the month concerned. Here, May is represented by a country ride in which women can be seen dressed in green, the colour of spring, with a man in blue at the centre of the image – perhaps the Duke himself, for whom the book was produced.

The Koran and the Islamic World

The Koran, or *al-Qur'ān*, is the holy book of Islam, considered by believers to be the miraculous revelation of God's own words to the prophet Mohammed. No other book in history has been so widely read in its original language.

Born in Mecca in 570 CE, Mohammed had no literary pedigree when, at the age of forty, he began to receive a series of revelations and to utter passages of rhyming, unmetred prophetic prose. As he gained followers, they memorized and recited the verses, which the prophet continued to bring forth at intervals until his death in 632 CE.

During Mohammed's lifetime, his revelations were transmitted orally from memory by specialist Koran-reciters. Textual standardization began under Caliph Abu Bakr (573–634), who organized the systematic collection of Mohammed's words in writing because he feared that the oral tradition could be lost following the deaths of a number of Koran-reciters in battle. However, the Koran had not yet acquired its final set form by the time the first copies were completed. One of Abu Bakr's successors, Caliph Uthman (r. 644–56), ordered all pre-existing texts to be burned once his authoritative version, the 'Uthmanic recension', had been compiled from a manuscript that he acquired from Hafsa, a wife of Mohammed. The earliest surviving Koranic manuscript fragments are from reputed Uthmanic originals written on parchment in the 650s; the oldest known complete volume dates to the ninth century.

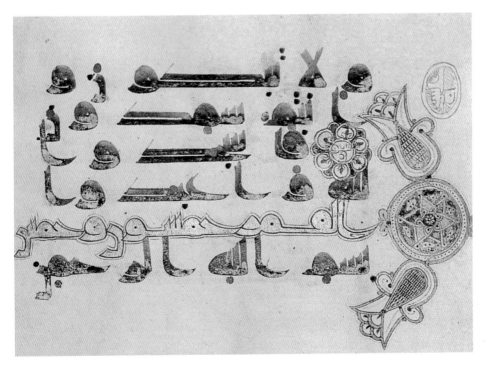

A verse from the Koran, in calligraphic Kufic script, which was used from the eighth to the tenth centuries. This manuscript on vellum comes from the Great Mosque of Kairouan in modern Tunisia. Calligraphy was used for copying sacred texts to honour the magnificence of God.

The Koran is of similar length to the New Testament. It is written in classical Arabic, which is read from right to left, with no capitals and no punctuation. The text is made up of 114 *suras*, sections varying from 10 to 6,100 words in length and arranged in a set sequence that shuns straightforward chronological narrative. There are two types of *sura*: Meccan and Medinan. The Meccan *suras* date from the prophet's time in Mecca and are dramatic and eschatological; those spoken after Mohammed fled with his followers to Medina describe how to live as a Muslim. *Suras* are divided into verse-like passages called *ayas* ('signs'). The Koran can be split into various divisions of even parts: during the holy month of Ramadan, for instance, one part of a thirty-part division is read out each day.

Muslims immediately adopted the modern codex for the Koran, with its parchment sheets bound or kept loose in a box. In Islamic tradition the physical book must be treated with utmost respect; it is usually protected by a case or a special bag as it must not come into contact with the ground or anything considered unclean, and readers must wash before touching it. For these reasons Islamic sacred codices have a flap attached to the back cover, which can be folded over to protect the whole front edge of the book.

This fifteenth-century Koran from Egypt has a flap-binding which enabled the reader to close the book completely for protection. The Koran has been ever-present in Muslim life and at the height of the Arab expansion it was used from Spain to China.

Although the Koran does not explicitly ban artistic depictions of humans or animals, pictorial representation in Islamic books has traditionally been limited in order to avoid idolatry. Books from Turkey, Iran and Mughal India, however, were often richly decorated with representational illustrations; elsewhere, artists used strands of tiny writing to construct lines and images. Calligraphy itself was considered a high art, even a test of character: an ancient Arabic proverb proclaims 'Purity of writing is purity of the soul', and the calligraphy of fine volumes of the Koran was highly prized, especially those produced by the celebrated scribe Hafiz Osman (d. 1698). Until the sixteenth century, the greatest centres of book artistry in the Islamic world were in Herat, in modern-day Afghanistan, and Tabriz and Shiraz, in what is now Iran.

Books underpinned the so-called 'golden age' of Islamic culture, from the eighth to the thirteenth century, when Arabic learning enjoyed global pre-eminence. As Islamic empires expanded, their new subjects were taught the language of the Koran, and written Arabic became the common language of communication. Muslim scholars and libraries collected and translated Western classical texts, and made great advances in philosophy, law, mathematics and the sciences.

The acquisition of paper technology from Chinese sailors captured in a battle of 751 aided the development of extensive libraries in the Islamic world. Baghdad had a paper mill by 791 and was later home to one of the three great Islamic libraries of the age. The Mongols were to destroy the city in 1258, but the libraries of Cairo and Cordoba would continue to flourish – the latter's collection reputedly held 400,000 volumes. The Mongol conqueror Timur (1336–1405, known in the West as 'Tamerlaine') and his successors established further great libraries in Persia, central Asia and India.

Despite this flourishing bibliophilia, printing with moveable type was not fully adopted by Islamic book-makers until the nineteenth century. Ottoman Sultan Bayazid II (r. 1481–1512) banned printed matter throughout the empire in 1485. The artistic, religious and moral importance attached to calligraphy may have been a significant factor in this decision, and with up to 100,000 Muslim copyists producing texts for scholars and libraries, there was no scarcity of books at the time. The law was repealed for secular works in 1727, but holy texts were withheld from the press for another hundred years. In the 1840s Mohammed Ali, Pasha of Egypt (1769–1849), incorporated printing into his projects for modernization. During the second half of the nineteenth century a Muslim print revolution made Beirut the important secular publishing centre it still is today.

Above: An Ottoman manuscript from the fourteenth century, showing the angel Gabriel who inspired Mohammed.

Below: A miniature *gubar* script, first invented to send messages via pigeons, and later adopted to copy miniature Korans in a codex or scroll. The text is enclosed within letters that form part of the verses.

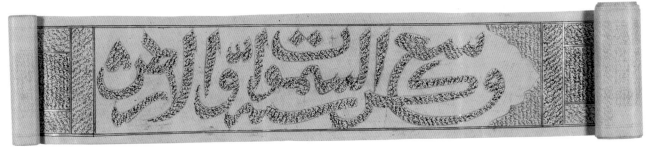

The Hebrew Book

The Dead Sea Scrolls are among the earliest surviving Jewish manuscripts. They consist of over 900 documents in Hebrew, Greek and Aramaic, mostly on parchment but some on papyrus, which were accidentally discovered by Bedouin shepherds in eleven caves near Khirbet Qumran, south of Jericho, between 1947 and 1956. They contain biblical texts and interpretations, apocryphal texts (books not included in canonical versions of the Jewish Bible) and other texts about community organization, written between about 200 BCE and 100 CE.

A fragment from the Dead Sea Scrolls containing the Songs of the Sabbath Sacrifice for the first thirteen Sabbaths of the year.

Another important cache of ancient Jewish manuscripts was found in a *genizah* (document store) in the Ben Ezra synagogue in Cairo at the end of the nineteenth century. Since in Jewish tradition a paper bearing the divine name cannot be destroyed, many worn-out Hebrew manuscripts and fragments had been put into permanent storage. The diverse collection of documents included rabbinical texts, historical accounts, and religious and secular poems, dating from the sixth century through the nineteenth century CE.

The Torah is the most sacred book in Judaism. It contains the text of the Five Books of Moses (Genesis, Exodus, Leviticus, Numbers and Deuteronomy), known in Greek as the Pentateuch. Orthodox Jews consider the words of the Torah to be of divine origin, communicated directly to Moses on Mount Sinai. The Torah, which is chanted by a specially trained reader during religious services, is always handwritten on a double parchment scroll according to strict ancient scribal requirements. It is treated with extreme reverence and must not be allowed to touch the ground. When not in use, the

Solomon Schechter studying documents at the Ben Ezra synagogue, Cairo, in 1896. Schechter (1847–1915) was a Moldavian-born rabbi and scholar who initiated the first scientific assessment of the documents found in the store room. Schechter spent twenty years in England and inspired the growth of British liberal Judaism.

Torah scrolls are stored in a protective ritual cabinet called an ark, which is the focal point of the synagogue. The scrolls are usually dressed with embroidered velvet coverings, miniature crowns and gold and silver finials adorned with bells.

The sacred books of Judaism also include the writings of the prophets (*nevi'im*) and other writings (*ketuvim*), among them the Psalms, Proverbs, Job and minor historical texts. Together these writings (known to Christians as the Old Testament) are called the *Tanach*. Orally transmitted law (*mishnah*) and commentaries on the Talmud are also considered by some Orthodox Jews to be divinely inspired. The Talmud consists of early rabbinical discussions of Jewish laws and customs, and is required reading in the traditional Jewish educational system.

For many medieval Jews, books were not essential to individual worship, as the texts that were chanted during religious services and ceremonies in the home were typically transmitted orally and memorized. However, books were available in the *yeshivah*, schools where young men studied for rabbinical ordination, and in the *beit midrash* ('House of Learning') attached to a synagogue. In this way the medieval synagogue

Above left: **Solomon reads the Torah in an illustration from the North French Hebrew Miscellany, a huge collection of Hebrew texts from the late thirteenth century. Putting all five books of the Torah on to a single scroll was a challenge for copyists.**

Above right: **A rabbi in prayer shawl reads the Torah from a ceremonial scroll in a synagogue. He follows the text holding a silver pointer (*yad*) so that his hand never touches the scroll.**

often functioned as a public library, where wealthy members of the community might deposit their books for public study.

In the Middle Ages, Hebrew books were hand-copied by individual scholars, as there was no Jewish equivalent of a monastic scriptorium. Jews, like Muslims, were reluctant to adopt printing for sacred texts. The first Hebrew printed book (Rashi's commentary on the Torah) appeared in Reggio di Calabria, Italy, in 1475. Anti-Semitic persecution frequently interfered with the production and distribution of Hebrew books. In 1241 the Talmud was publicly burned for the first time in Paris, a practice that would continue periodically for several centuries. In fifteenth-century Venice, Christian censors routinely purged Hebrew books of anything that offended Christian belief.

Spain was an important region for Hebrew book production until Jews were expelled from the Iberian peninsula in 1492, after which Venice became the centre of the industry. In the seventeenth century Amsterdam took over as the main city for the production and export of Hebrew books. In the late eighteenth and early nineteenth centuries, central and eastern European cities such as Vienna, Warsaw, Lvov and Vilnius became centres of publishing that supported the *Haskalah*, the movement for Jewish Enlightenment.

By the nineteenth century, there existed not only an elite of Torah scholars but also a broad Jewish secular readership and intelligentsia. A renaissance of Hebrew publishing between 1890 and 1920 was inspired by the Zionist movement, which supported the revival of Hebrew language and literature. Among the most successful publishing houses was Tushiyah, founded in Warsaw in 1896 by Avraham Leib Shalkovich (better known by his pseudonym 'Ben-Avigdor', 1866–1921), which produced secular Hebrew-language popular titles, classics, literature, children's books and scientific texts, as well as a number of important works in Yiddish (the everyday spoken language of eastern European Jews).

The Golden Haggadah, produced in medieval Spain, is a richly illustrated manuscript copy of the liturgical book used by Jewish households on the eve of Passover. This page depicts scenes from the Book of Exodus and the liberation of the Israelites. The panels at the top right show the plague of the first-born; at the bottom left, Moses watches the drowning of the Egyptians, portrayed as medieval knights.

2 THE NEW CULTURE OF PRINT

Technological advances such as the invention of moveable type do not happen out of the blue. When Gutenberg invented printing in the 1440s it was not a 'Eureka!' moment like the one Archimedes is supposed to have had in his bath, but the outcome of a cumulative process of technological innovation. Gutenberg was part of a team; he developed his printing press in response to a rising demand for books and was supported by long-term investors.

Although some aspects of book production remained the same as in the age of the scriptoria, printing brought potentially faster production and encouraged the standardization of Europe's major languages. The printing press itself was relatively cheap; the greatest expense of book production until the eighteenth century was paper, the cost of which might amount to over half of a book's retail price. It was still made according to methods learned from the Arabs, from rags and discarded cloth, collected by poor 'ragpickers' all over Europe. The physical form of the book – the codex – was unchanged, and would remain so for more than 500 years.

Printing had many detractors, who feared it would spread lies and subversion. In their eyes, print had the power to corrupt undiscerning readers and to spread heresy more widely than ever before.

Printing equipment from Christopher Plantin's shop in Antwerp: a hand press and blocks of type, inking ball, sheets hung up to dry and the typesetter's cases in the background. In the foreground are early editions published by Aldus Manutius.

Gutenberg and his Bible

Johannes Gensfleisch zur Laden zum Gutenberg, better known as Gutenberg, is something of a mysterious figure. Few hard facts are known about his life, apart from a lawsuit for breach of promise that was brought against him in the 1430s. The invention of printing is nevertheless attributed to him, at some time in the 1440s in the German city of Mainz, even though it is not clear exactly when he settled there; Strasbourg, where he had previously worked for over a decade, also claims to be the crucible of printing.

The invention of printing from moveable type was, in practice, a whole series of inventions. First the matrices or moulds had to be made, and from these metal characters of the desired strength and consistency had to be forged. The formula for an indelible, oil-based ink had to be perfected. Then the hand press itself had to be designed and manufactured. Developing each of these elements required time, teamwork and investment capital. Gutenberg was supported for years by his financial partners, Johann Fust and Peter Schöffer. Perhaps inevitably, he ran into debt and was forced to surrender ownership of his workshop to Fust. Three hundred years later, in 1740, Fust and Schöffer were still being named as the inventors of the printing press, along with their mere 'associate' Gutenberg.

A woodcut portrait of Johannes Gutenberg, engraved by Nicolas de Larmessin and published in Jacques Ignace Bullart's *Académie des sciences et des arts*, Paris, 1682. The accompanying text described him as the inventor of printing. Common variations of his surname were Gudenberger, Gudenberg and Guttemberg.

Other circumstances converged to bring about the emergence of moveable type in Germany in the mid-fifteenth century. Demand for books was increasing. Humanist scholarship and the spread of universities created a larger market for books among both the secular and religious intellectual elites. The rise of cities and commercial centres created another consumer market in the form of judicial, administrative and clerical institutions with a high demand for printed materials. The production of hand-copied books was already accelerating to meet some of this demand before the 1440s. Technological developments also made Gutenberg's work possible. For a decade he had worked in Strasbourg as a jeweller, cutting precious stones and producing mirrors to sell to pilgrims en route to Aachen. The metal industries had made significant advances in Germany, and conditions were ripe for Gutenberg's experiments in forging moveable type. He spent years of trial and error to find the best combinations for his matrices and characters, trying lead, antimony, copper and tin in different proportions.

Gutenberg probably printed the 42-line Bible that bears his name in Mainz in the mid-1450s. The typesetting and printing of the Gutenberg Bible took over two years. But whereas a scribe would have taken three years to produce a single copy, Gutenberg made 180, about 150 of them on paper and 30 on vellum, which would have required about 5,000 calfskins. His first ink was made of soot from lamps, mixed with varnish and egg whites; he tried many chemical mixtures to produce the distinctively rich black ink of the Gutenberg Bible. Each page was individually rubricated (capital letters were

Above: The Mainz Psalter which was commissioned by the Archbishop of Mainz in 1457, typeset for the first page. This was perhaps only the second book to be printed with moveable type, and it combined printed text with two-colour woodcuts. The psalter was printed on vellum using black and red inks, with large coloured capitals in red and blue and music written in flowing script.

Left: The Gutenberg Bible was the first book produced with moveable type in Europe. Working from St Jerome's Vulgate, Gutenberg produced a two-volume Bible in severe double-column text. There were no paragraph breaks or page numbers. This is the opening of the Book of Proverbs' from the British Library's paper copy, volume 2.

touched up by hand in red ink) and illuminated, so that they all were subtly different. Experts know the Gutenberg Bible as 'B-42', for its regular 42 lines per page. But Gutenberg started with only 40 lines, extending this to 42 lines by page 11, probably to economize on paper.

Although Gutenberg is often lauded as a Protestant hero in the tradition of John Wycliffe and Martin Luther for his role in making the text of the Bible more widely accessible, in the early world of print the Catholic Church was by far the biggest customer and supplier of content. Gutenberg knew which side his bread was buttered. In the 1450s he printed papal indulgences to raise money for the defence of Cyprus against the Turks. The sale of papal indulgences was one of the very practices that Luther had strenuously attacked.

Gutenberg was not the first inventor of moveable type. Xylographic woodcut printing – sometimes using moveable characters – was in use in China by the eleventh century and Korea by the thirteenth. Two hundred years before Gutenberg's invention, Koreans had produced what were probably the first moveable characters made from metal, but this technology did not come into widespread use in East Asia. In China, for example, mass print production was not a priority, as there was no real market for books outside the emperor's palace. Moreover, the existing wood-based printing technology was suited to Chinese and Korean paper, for it did not demand the forceful downward pressure of a heavy platen on to a metal plate that was needed to leave an ink impression on the stiffer European paper.

Although printing first appeared in Asia, it was in Europe that printing was to have widespread social and cultural consequences, and the printing press itself was a Western invention. Gutenberg knew nothing about the achievements of the Koreans: through his efforts, printing was reinvented in Europe.

Below: Metal type was used in Korean printing before Gutenberg. This work of Collected Commentaries on the Spring and Autumn Annals (historical texts) was produced in 1434.

How Printers Worked

Type composition demanded speed, skill and dexterity – like touch-typing – not to mention a good knowledge of Latin. First, the compositor assembled the characters by hand from the cases in which they were stored in rectangular compartments. With the written text pinned up in front of him, he faced the case, which was arranged on a sloping surface for easy access. The case would usually be divided into two, with the capital letters in the upper section and ordinary letters in the lower section (hence the terms 'upper case' and 'lower case'). The compositor prepared several lines at a time in a metal composing stick held in one hand. Once they were complete, he arranged these lines in pages in a wooden frame called a galley, wedging in the characters with small pieces of wood to ensure they did not get displaced.

When the correct number of pages had been composed, the galleys were laid face up in a frame or 'forme' on a flat stone or marble surface. A rail allowed the printer to slide the stone and the forme back and forth like a trolley, so that new pages could quickly

In this *Danse macabre*, printed by Mathias Huss in Lyon in 1499, the skeleton of death visits a printing workshop, with a compositor seated at the left, printers with press and inking ball and the bookseller at the counter.

The many crafts and trades that Gutenberg's invention brought in its train are illustrated in a series of sixteenth-century woodcuts by Jost Amman. Depicted here are the paper-maker and the type-founder.

replace those already printed. Ink was then applied to the characters by hand with a leather ink-ball, and a sheet of dampened paper was laid over the forme. The paper was held in a hinged frame called a 'tympan' and secured with a 'frisket', a second frame made of parchment, which also protected the margins of the paper from ink stains. The printers, usually working in pairs, then lowered the platen, a heavy horizontal pressing surface, over the pages by means of a lever and screw mechanism. The downward pressure exerted by the platen transferred the ink from the type to the underside of the paper. The platen had to be exactly parallel to the stone surface; otherwise the pressure exerted would be uneven and some parts of the page would be more clearly printed than others. After printing, the pages were hung up to dry.

If both black and red were being used on the same folio, the whole process had to be repeated with a different-coloured ink. Only one side of the paper could be printed at once, but skilled workers could produce a page every 20 seconds. Proofreading, if any, was rudimentary: the printer would check the printed pages as they came off the press. In spite of its imperfections, this system was remarkably enduring. In terms of printing technology, the age of Gutenberg lasted until the early nineteenth century – over three hundred years.

The hand-driven wooden printing press was not expensive, but the metal characters that went with it were a considerable investment, and printers were always keen to snap up a second-hand set if a bankrupt colleague's equipment went up for auction. A print shop might need fonts in Latin and Greek as well as the vernacular, and possibly Hebrew if it produced multilingual Bibles. It was a specialized and time-consuming job to make the punches and then the matrices from which metal characters were formed.

The printer needed to draw on a stock of several hundred thousand characters, otherwise he would be able to compose only a few pages at a time and the type would wear out quickly from overuse.

The master printer of the sixteenth century had to be multi-skilled. He was not merely a printer, but also a bookseller, a capitalist entrepreneur, an indexer and a translator familiar with several languages, as well as a proofreader and copyeditor. He needed to be on good terms with eminent scholars on one hand, and wealthy patrons and rulers on the other. His special contribution to intellectual life should not be underestimated.

Printers were organized into highly regulated guilds. In England, the Stationers' Company received a royal charter in 1557 to oversee the English book trade and prevent seditious printing. The Company's role was to regulate and discipline the industry, define proper conduct and maintain its own corporate privileges. It held a number of monopoly franchises on the production of Bibles, law books and educational texts. It also held a royal privilege to produce almanacs. This business was called the English Stock. Members of the Stationers' Company could own shares in it and receive dividends accordingly; the printing work and a portion of the profits were allocated to the Company's poorest members. The English Stock was a major income-earner and the Stationers' Company defended it doggedly against piracy from unauthorized publishers.

Amman woodcuts showing a compositor with his composing stick and two-page forme, and printers and bookbinders at work.

Printing Conquers the World

Gutenberg's workers, who led a semi-nomadic existence, were offered commissions by great aristocrats, universities and the law courts. The invention was first taken up in the busy commercial cities situated in the economic hub of Western Europe, in the Netherlands, Germany and the Rhineland, and in northern Italy, where Venice dominated the book trade. By 1480, 110 towns had a printing press and by 1500, the number of centres had more than doubled to 236.

The printing press took a little longer to reach Britain, although thriving commercial connections between southern England and the Low Countries meant that its arrival in London was not long delayed. William Caxton, the first English printer, produced the first English-language printed book while working in Bruges in 1474. He moved to London, where he set up shop, with royal patronage, in the vicinity of Westminster Abbey. Paris had its Latin Quarter, close to the Sorbonne, which became the

The second edition of Geoffrey Chaucer's *Canterbury Tales*, printed by William Caxton in 1483. Woodcuts depicted each pilgrim on horseback: the Merchant on the left and the Clerk of Oxford on the right. Some images were reused to illustrate other pilgrims, which explains why the 'clerk' is armed with bow and arrows.

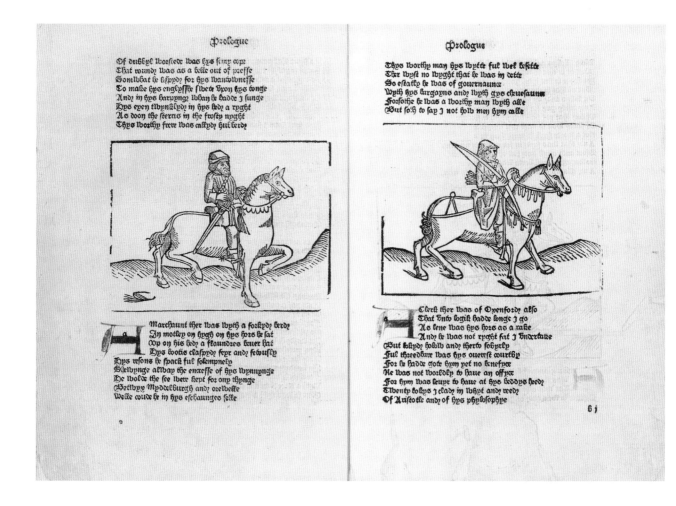

headquarters of the French book trade; London had Paternoster Row, where printers gathered in the area near St Paul's cathedral, conveniently close to the law courts that constantly demanded printed works.

In Switzerland, Basle and Geneva (where many Calvinists took refuge) were important printing centres, while in Spain the printing press found a home in Toledo, which was a great ecclesiastical centre, in Valladolid, home of the royal court, and in Alcalá de Henares, with its university. In France, the publishing industry was divided between the capital and Lyon. In 1530, these two cities produced 90 per cent of all French books. Paris became the publishing hub of the Counter-Reformation, churning out liturgical works and books of hours; Lyon specialized in supplying the Italian and Spanish markets.

First printing spread throughout Europe; then the printing press became an essential companion to the Europeanization of the world. In the sixteenth century, eastern Europe and the Nordic countries acquired their first printing presses. Moscow had a press by the 1560s, and Ljubljana by the 1570s. There was a press in Constantinople by 1727. The press reached North America in 1638, when it arrived in New England. The Spanish conquerors established a printing press in Mexico in 1539, but it was never allowed to compete with imported books from Spain; local presses in the New World were set up only to assist missionaries in the conversion of local peoples. By 1580, printing had reached Lima, and in 1590 Jesuit missionaries took it to Japan. In 1593, the Spanish brought a press to Manila, the first in South-east Asia. A printing press arrived in Australia with the first convict fleet in 1788. Napoleon brought the press to Egypt in 1798, together with Greek and Arabic type and an impressive cohort of scientists and intellectuals.

This dictionary produced by the friar Alonso de Molina in 1550 was one of the earliest Spanish-language books printed in Mexico. This edition only contained the section for Spanish to Nahuatl (the language spoken by the indigenous Nahua people); Alonso added a Nahuatl to Spanish section twenty years later. The first page shows St Francis receiving the stigmata.

The *Historia de la Provincia del Sancto Rosario*, by Diego de Aduarte, was printed in Manila in 1640 in folio format on fragile rice paper. It was the first major historical work printed in the Spanish colony.

Print runs were still comparatively limited. Titles were customarily produced in editions of between 500 and 1,500 copies right up to the nineteenth century. Cheap, popular titles such as catechisms and almanacs were, however, produced in vast editions of tens of thousands of copies. These would be bound cheaply, in rough paper, but more expensive books were very often not bound at all. Transporting unbound paper was cheaper, and booksellers were unwilling to invest in expensive binding unless they were certain of making a sale. They expected the customer to provide his or her own personalized binding.

Latin and the Vernaculars

In Europe, Latin was the language of law, science and the Church. Latin books accounted for 77 per cent of all books printed before 1501 (known as the *incunabula*, from the Latin for 'cradle'). Initially, the invention of printing vastly increased production of books in Latin, especially religious books for the established Church. In 1546, the Council of Trent affirmed that the Latin Vulgate Bible was the only authentic version of scripture. In the 1570s, 70 per cent of books published in Germany were still in Latin, and about three-quarters were religious works. Latin was a lingua franca that made it possible for educated people from different nations and cultures to communicate. When Galileo Galilei (1564–1642) began writing his scientific books in Italian instead of Latin in the

Frontispiece and title page of a 1534 edition of William Tindall's (Tyndale's) English New Testament, possibly published in Antwerp by Merten de Keyser. Two years later the author was burned at the stake as a heretic in Flanders.

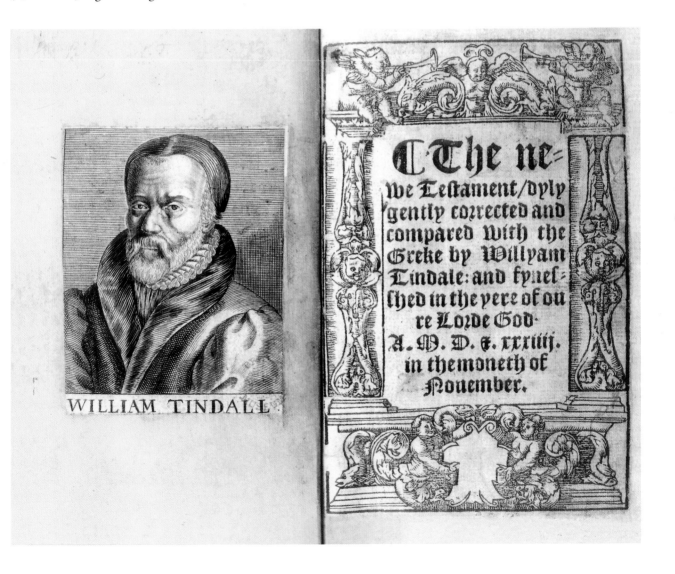

WILLIAM TINDALL

The newe Testament/dylygently corrected and compared with the Greke by Willyam Tindale: and fynesshed in the yere of oure Lorde God·A. M. D. E. rrriiij. in the moneth of Nouember.

second decade of the seventeenth century, there were many complaints from his international readers.

Nevertheless, the supremacy of Latin was gradually eroded by two powerful currents. One was the independent power of sovereign states, which saw political advantage in promoting their own national languages, and the other was Protestantism. In 1539, the French king François I issued the decree of Villers-Cotterêts, which made French rather than Latin the language of all official documents, although most of his subjects were still unable to read either. In England, the dissolution of the monasteries (1536–41), in the wake of Henry VIII's brawl with the papacy, severely weakened Latin print culture by undermining one of the greatest sources of patronage for Latin book production. In fact, no significant Latin works were printed in England for almost a century, and in 1625 the Stationers' Company deleted all its Latin stock.

The Protestant Reformation encouraged the spread of vernacular languages in print. The message of the Bible, Protestant leaders believed, should be accessible to all Christians, in their own languages. The first major printed text to be translated from Latin into vernacular languages was the Bible. Usually the New Testament came first, because it was shorter than the Old, easier to translate and more central to everyday Christian theology. A Dutch Bible appeared in 1526, the same year that William Tyndale's English version of the New Testament reached England from the Continent. Forty editions of the Dutch Bible were published over the next forty years. Many French-language Bibles were imported to France from Lutheran centres such as Strasbourg and Calvinist centres such as Geneva. The first domestically produced French New Testament was published in 1523 by Lefèvre d'Étaples; over the next decade he managed to produce an entire Bible. In the early days of the Protestant Reformation it was politically risky to produce vernacular Bibles as the Catholic Church considered them heretical, and governments associated them with seditious movements. In England, Tyndale's Bible was burned repeatedly, and he himself died at the stake in 1536.

In 1541, however, when Henry's Reformation was more politically secure, the English monarchy began to regard vernacular Bibles as useful instruments in encouraging national unity and consolidating royal supremacy over the Church, and ordered that every parish church should provide itself with a copy. In 1611, the King James Authorized Version appeared, displacing earlier English-language translations. But it cost as much as £2, which was prohibitively expensive, unless the reader bought individual sections, or one of the smaller, condensed versions that were known as 'thumb Bibles'.

Opposite: The Dutch Bible of 1526, translated by the Antwerp printer Jacob van Liesvelt (*c.* 1490–1545), relied heavily on Luther's New Testament. The Protestant Reformation encouraged publication of the scriptures in vernacular languages, although the Catholic Church and several rulers found this dangerously radical.

Below: The first page of the New Testament of Lefèvre d'Étaples's first complete French Bible, translated from the Vulgate and published in 1530. Since vernacular Bibles were still banned in France this edition was published in Antwerp, under a privilege granted by Emperor Charles V.

Luther's Bible

Martin Luther's German Bible holds a special place in Reformation history. More than any other book, it represented the Lutheran ideal of the 'priesthood of all believers', a world in which ordinary people could consult the word of God for themselves, without the guidance and interpretation of the clergy. And yet, in practice, the spread of Lutheranism relied on publications other than the German Bible, which, because of its cost, was not yet within the reach of all believers.

The title page to the full German edition of Luther's *Wittenberg Bible*, printed in 1534 in two quarto volumes by Hans Lufft, with illuminations by Lucas Cranach. Lufft went on to print more than 100,000 copies over the next forty years.

A 1538 broadside against the Catholic Church with a hand-coloured woodcut from the workshop of Lucas Cranach, a satirical coat of arms for the Pope, and text by Martin Luther. The two broken keys suggest that the Pope's hold on the world is at an end.

Luther's Bible was not unique: there had been eighteen other German versions before his. But these earlier translations tended to produce very literal renderings of the original text. Unlike the efforts of his predecessors, Luther's translation was accessible to speakers of many local German dialects. In 1522 he first produced a New Testament in German. It had taken him only eleven weeks to translate, and it came off the presses within six months. It was reprinted fourteen times in Wittenberg within its first two years of publication, and dozens more editions appeared in Augsburg, Leipzig, Strasbourg and Basle. Translating the Old Testament into German was much more difficult, and it took Luther another twelve years to complete the job.

Luther's Bible was a bestseller of its time. About 200,000 copies in hundreds of reprinted editions appeared before Luther himself died in 1546. But the book remained too expensive for most Lutherans, and at that time only 3 or 4 per cent of Germans were able to read anyway. An unbound copy of the complete German Bible of 1534 cost the equivalent of a month's wages for the average labourer. The German Bible was bought, as Luther intended, by churches, pastors and schools. The governments of some German principalities boosted sales and circulation by ordering every priest and parish to own one – this was the case, for example, in Hessen and Brandenburg.

The ideal of putting a German Bible into every peasant's cottage could not yet become a reality. The situation was different in Scandinavia and the Calvinist

Netherlands, where the ability to read (though not necessarily to write) was more widespread. In these areas, printers found it profitable to produce small-format octavo editions, which were portable and could be used by ordinary families. There was approximately one Bible in circulation for every twenty-five Dutch speakers between 1520 and 1566. In seventeenth-century New England, Bible ownership was probably also much more common than it was in early modern Germany.

The German Bible, then, was not the chief messenger of Lutheranism. The movement kept printers busy with the production of a mass of pamphlets, brochures, catechisms and one-page broadsheets (*Flugschriften*, or 'flysheets'), and the enemies of the Reformation responded in kind, producing a massive pamphlet war. The *Flugschriften* included crude woodcut images which carried Luther's messages to the illiterate, depicting the papacy as the Whore of Babylon, Luther as the Good Shepherd and the clergy as corrupt and decadent. About three million pamphlets circulated in Germany between 1518 and 1525 – the entire population of Germany was then only 13 million. Luther's *Appeal to the Christian Nobility of the German Nation* (1520) had a print run of 4,000 copies and sold out in a few days. It had a further sixteen editions.

Like many other sixteenth-century authors, Luther was dismayed to find that he had lost control of his own publications. His works were pirated all over Germany and Switzerland by unscrupulous printers, who caught the scent of a good profit. In the process, his texts were abridged, altered and distorted. In the early world of print, it was futile for an author to brand any version of his text as illegitimate – someone would print it regardless, and with impunity.

Martin Luther's *De Captivitate Babylonica Ecclesiae* (On the Babylonian Captivity of the Church), 1520, was a tract written in Latin against the Pope and in favour of reducing the number of sacraments. Soon afterwards Luther was excommunicated.

Books of the Scientific Revolution

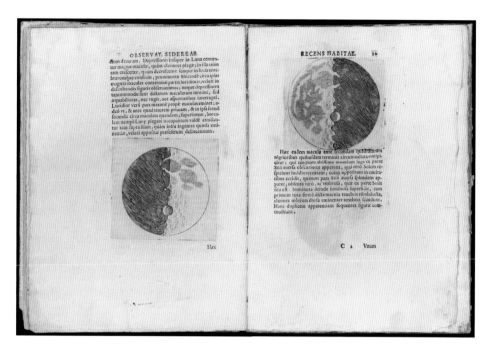

Before the advent of the printing press there was no mass market in Europe for scientific treatises, as there had been for religious books. Printing decisively changed the way scientific knowledge was communicated. For one thing, it enabled accurate diagrams, maps, anatomical drawings and representations of flora and fauna to be reproduced. Previously, woodcut illustrations had deteriorated with repetitive use, but with the development of engraved metal plates accurate visual information was made more permanent. This was a slow process, and printers' blunders still often resulted in the spread of false data. In Galileo's *Sidereus Nuncius* (The Starry Messenger), published in Venice in 1610, his telescopic images of the lunar surface appeared back to front.

Printing also made scholarly books more widely accessible, allowing researchers to consult ancient texts freely and to compare their own observations with those of fellow scholars. The Danish aristocrat and astronomer Tycho Brahe (1546–1601), for instance, was able to buy the writings of the classical astronomer Ptolemy (*c.* 90–*c.* 168 CE) and Nicolaus Copernicus (1473–1543) in sixteenth-century Copenhagen; he did not have to start from scratch in making sense of his own observational data. Brahe installed printing presses and a paper mill on his private island of Hven to produce his own self-published treatises,

bypassing normal commercial constraints. Brahe's former assistant, the German scholar Johannes Kepler (1571–1630), succeeded him as imperial mathematician, and discovered that the orbits of the planets were not perfectly circular, but elliptical. Kepler personally oversaw the production of his *Tabulae Rudolphinae*, based on Brahe's observations and published in Ulm in 1627. Kepler designed his own frontispiece, an elaborate engraving depicting himself in the company of Copernicus and the great astronomers of antiquity, and took the work to the Frankfurt Book Fair of 1627.

Scientists needed royal or aristocratic patronage; in 1632, Galileo dedicated his *Dialogue on Two Chief World Systems* to his patron Ferdinand II de' Medici. This, however, did not protect him from prosecution by the Inquisition. Scientists who wanted to publish their findings frequently had to negotiate repression by the Catholic Church. In 1616, the work of Copernicus was declared contrary to Holy Scripture, but in 1617, Willem Janszoon Blaeu (1571–1653), a maker of celestial globes in Amsterdam, produced a new edition of Copernicus's controversial *De revolutionibus orbium coelestium* (On the Revolutions of the Heavenly Spheres), originally published in 1543. Protestant publishers could profit from titles banned by Catholic authorities. Kepler's *Epitome astronomiae Copernicanae* (1617) was put on the Index of Prohibited Books. In 1633 Galileo was convicted of heresy, forced to retract his ideas and put under house arrest. But his *Discourses and Mathematical Demonstrations Concerning Two New Sciences* was smuggled into a diplomatic bag and printed by Elzevir in Leiden in 1638. Publication was usually easier in Protestant countries. In London, for instance, the Royal Society, licensed to print in 1662, disseminated much new scientific work in the pages of its Transactions.

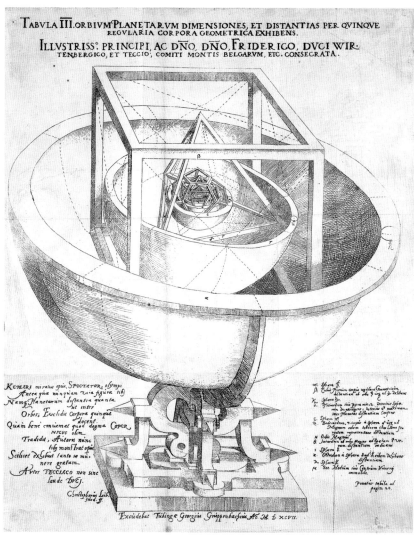

This diagram of the planetary spheres from Johannes Kepler's *Tabulae Rudolphinae* shows how the astronomer modelled the universe. His work provided the data for computing the positions of the planets with sufficient accuracy to predict the transit of Mercury in 1631.

Atlases and Cartography

Until the sixteenth century, maps of the world were still based on classical Greek models, in particular on Ptolemy's *Geographia* (*c.* 150 CE). Ptolemy had tried to tackle the problem of producing a two-dimensional representation of a spherical object – our planet – but greatly underestimated the size of the earth. This miscalculation later led Christopher Columbus (1451–1506) to believe he could reach Asia more quickly by sailing west from Europe, rather than east.

In the great age of exploration, Europeans' knowledge of world geography grew more extensive. Flemish cartographer Abraham Ortelius's *Theatrum orbis terrarum*, first published in Antwerp in 1570, was the first modern atlas. It included sixty-nine maps covering the whole world, and summarized the enormous advances in cartography that Europe had made. It was frequently revised, supplemented and re-edited.

Ortelius (1527–98) depicted a large southern continent lying to the south of Africa and South America, straddling the Indian and Pacific Oceans. This was 'Terra Australis

Abraham Ortelius's world map of 1570, showing a vast southern continent and a strangely shaped South American continent.

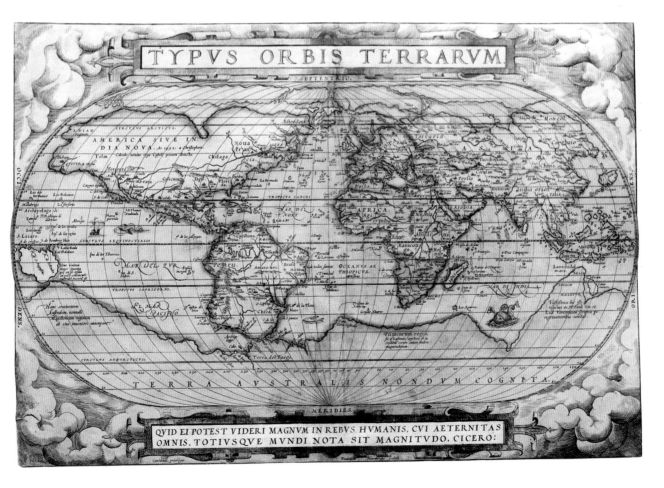

The first 'map' of Australia, originally drawn in 1547 by Nicolas Vallard. It shows the east coast with the south at the top. As with many contemporary maps, some local inhabitants and marine life were depicted.

Nondum Cognita' ('the southern land as yet unknown'). A great southern land mass was assumed to exist because it was thought that the continents of the northern hemisphere needed a counterweight to keep the earth balanced. Until the Age of Enlightenment, this notion encouraged speculation, fantasy and wildly inaccurate mapping. James Cook charted the coasts of New Zealand and eastern Australia on his first voyage (1768–71), but a larger continent was still thought to exist further south. On his second journey (1772–75) he sailed on towards the Antarctic and scotched the myth once and for all, finding absolutely nothing there. The French were to produce the first complete map of Australia, following the expedition of Nicolas Baudin in 1800–3.

Until the seventeenth century, maps often plagiarized each other, reproducing errors and imaginative fantasies about exotic lands received at third- or fourth-hand. Pieter van der Aa (1659–1733), for instance, published atlases in Leiden using the accounts of explorers in the Portuguese East Indies in the 1580s as a basis, but still including illustrations of the monstrous creatures that were traditionally believed to inhabit unexplored territories. Bernhard von Breydenbach (1440–97), a canon of Mainz cathedral, was one of the first to present topographical views recorded at first-hand by an objective eyewitness. During his journey to the Holy Land in 1483–84, he was accompanied by an artist, Erhard Reuwich, who produced a map and illustrations for his *Peregrinatio in Terram Sanctam*, which was published in 1486. This trend towards the realistic mapping of the earth eventually encouraged more accurate mapping of the heavens. For his *Selenographia*, published in 1647, the Polish-born astronomer Johannes Hevelius (1611–87) was the first to produce a detailed map of the moon's surface, pitted with craters, based on his own observations through a telescope.

The Printed Page

In the early world of print, books still closely resembled hand-copied manuscripts. New typography soon developed, however, and the information on the printed page began to include all the elements that we now take for granted.

Early printed books offered a rich introductory apparatus. At the beginning, there was an engraved frontispiece, often highly decorated and perhaps in the form of an archway welcoming the reader inside. An engraved portrait of the author might follow; through these images the portraits of Luther and Erasmus have become quite familiar. Books often had long titles that were a kind of advertisement for the contents, with a Latin or biblical quote added. When Thomas Salusbury published his translation of the text we know as Galileo's *Two Chief World Systems* in 1711, for example, the title read: *The Systeme of the World: in four dialogues. Wherein the two grand Systemes of Ptolomy and Copernicus are largely discoursed of; and the Reasons, both Phylosophical and Physical, as well as on one side as the other, impartially and indefinitely propounded, by Galileus Galileus Linceus, A Gentleman of Florence; Extraordinary Professor of the Mathematicks in the University of Pisa, and Chief Mathematician to the Grand Duke of Tuscany. Inglished from the original Italian copy, by Thomas Salusbury,* followed by mottos from Alcinous and Seneca. It also became customary to identify the printer, together with the place and date of publication, at the start of the book. This printer's signature was known as the colophon; in hand-copied books the equivalent device had come at the end of the text, where the scribe often signed his work. There might also be a letter dedicated to the author's patron, and only after this would the reader come to the table of contents.

Early printed books, like handwritten manuscripts, usually did not have page numbers – the reader was expected to add these by hand. Gradually, however, the printed book began to include these elements, along with running headers at the top of the page. Manuscript readers had added their own markers in the margin of the text, drawing symbols such as a bird or a hand with a

Frontispiece to Bernardus Mallinckrodt's *De ortu et progressu artis typographicae* (On the rise and progress of the art of printing). Mallinckrodt invented the term *incunabula* to denote European books printed before 1501. He defended Gutenberg (pictured on the left) in his claim to be the inventor of printing.

pointing index finger to indicate a passage of special interest. The printed book also incorporated such conventions.

Paragraph breaks had not been the norm before the sixteenth century, and so readers had faced seamless blocks of text, divided, if at all, into two columns of print. Those whose reading competence was not perfect needed well-ventilated texts, even if this forced printers to consume more of that most valuable commodity, paper. The Bible had been divided into books, chapters and verses in scribal culture, but there had been no uniform system accepted by all. The biblical divisions organized by the French printer Robert Estienne (Robertus Stephanus) in 1551 were eventually adopted universally.

Print brought standardization in place of the many variants and errors that inevitably characterized scribal copies. A clear sign of the new expectation that all versions of a text would conform to the original was the practice of the German humanist Erasmus (1466–1536), who issued *errata* slips, extra leaves correcting any errors, which could be bound in with the rest of the pages after the unbound book was sold.

Above left: The colophon, or printer's mark, of Andrew Myllar, who became Scotland's first authorized printer in 1507. The windmill logo refers to his surname.

Above right: The opening page of the Gospel according to Matthew in the French New Testament, printed by Robert Estienne in Geneva, 1553, showing chapter and verse divisions which became standard.

Aldus Manutius and the Classics

Renaissance readers and publishers helped to modernize the book, but did so, paradoxically, by looking backwards in time to the classical authors of Greek and Roman antiquity. Cicero was required reading for anyone wishing to understand law and politics, while the great poets Ovid, Virgil and Horace were literary benchmarks for all educated readers. Plato and Aristotle formed the bases of most philosophical commentaries, and Pliny was regarded as the leading authority on natural science.

The 'italic' type used by Aldus Manutius in this 1501 edition of Virgil's *Eclogues* aspired to simplicity and clarity in the classical style.

Small-format, easily portable versions of the classics were produced in octavo for a cultivated lay readership. One important pioneer of this revival of classical literature was the Venetian printer Aldus Manutius (1449–1515). For his series of pocket-sized editions of the classics, Manutius designed a new font, in which the letters were inclined, which he called 'italic' in reference to classical Italy. Although he tried to have the new font patented, he could not stop printers outside Venice from copying it.

The so-called 'Aldine classics', first produced in 1501–2, constituted a publishing revolution, although it was far from being a prototype for a paperback revolution, as the series was not cheap. Manutius aimed his series at a cultivated lay readership. The works of classical Latin authors such as Horace and Virgil, as well as Italian vernacular poets such as Petrarch and Dante, appeared in simple and elegant script without the encumbrance of notes or the distraction of scholarly commentary, which had been typical of classical literature during the Middle Ages.

Elzevir and the 'Dutch Miracle'

In the seventeenth century, a small European country with a population of under two million became a publishing powerhouse. Modern historians of the book describe this transformation as the 'Dutch miracle' that turned cities such as The Hague, Utrecht, Amsterdam and Leiden into important intellectual centres.

The Low Countries had several factors in their favour. The Dutch welcomed Calvinist refugees from the Spanish Netherlands, and many of them were printers. Without the severe censorship restrictions that prevailed in some other European states, a climate of tolerance reigned. In addition, the Dutch themselves enjoyed a high rate of literacy. Dutch entrepreneurs could take advantage of well-developed commercial networks, which helped to make seventeenth-century Holland into a great centre for the production of news, Bibles, political pamphlets and other printed literature.

The Elzevirs were one of the most eminent dynasties of the Dutch book trade. In 1580, Louis Elzevir (1540–1617), a former apprentice of Christopher Plantin in Antwerp, had moved to Leiden, where he founded his own business. His descendants printed textbooks, academic dissertations and classical texts for the University of Leiden.

The House of Elzevir issued its most acclaimed editions between 1622 and 1652, under the tenure of Bonaventure and Abraham Elzevir. They began to publish a series of

Below left: Title page of Elzevir's 1638 edition of Galileo Galilei's *Discorsi e dimostrazioni matematiche* (Discourses and Mathematical Demonstrations), published in Leiden with Elzevir's famous elm-tree logo.

Below right: Elzevir's business relied on reprints of the classics such as the works of Virgil. Opposite the title page of this 1636 edition is the owner's ex-libris on the left.

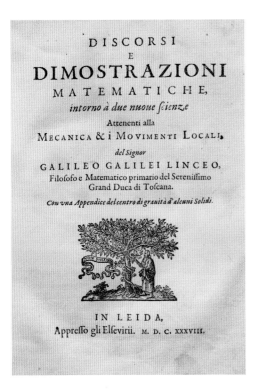

classical Latin texts in small duodecimo format, annotated by contemporary scholars. These pocket editions of the classics were quality products: scholarly, reliable and reasonably priced. The 1636 edition of Virgil's complete works was such a success that it was reprinted fifteen times. Pocket-sized classics quickly became known as 'elzevir editions', whether or not the Elzevirs were actually the publishers.

Bonaventure and Abraham Elzevir launched another bestselling series, the *Republics*, published in Latin between 1626 and 1649. Each volume gave information on the geography, inhabitants, economy and history of a country in Europe, Asia, Africa or the Near East. The *Republics* were the ancestors of modern travel guides.

The profits of such successes enabled the Elzevirs to finance riskier and more costly ventures. They produced Erasmus's version of the New Testament in seven editions from 1624 to 1678, six editions of Descartes's *Opera philosophica*, and Galileo's controversial *Discourses and Mathematical Demonstrations Concerning Two New Sciences* (1638), which was smuggled out of Italy, where Galileo was banned from publishing by the Inquisition. The Elzevirs also earned a reputation for typesetting in non-Roman alphabets at a time when the study of Semitic languages was flourishing in the Netherlands.

The Elzevir dynasty died out in 1712 and the 'Dutch miracle' waned as international competition gained ground on the Dutch book trade. But the name was revived in 1880 when Jacobus Robbers named his new publishing company 'Elsevier' and adopted the printer's logo used by Isaac Elzevir (1596–1651), which featured an old man standing beneath an elm, the tree of knowledge. By the mid-twentieth century, the company was publishing scientific journals and had branches in the Netherlands, the USA and the UK. In the 1970s it specialized in medical publishing. Today it survives as part of the Reed–Elsevier conglomerate, a leading provider of scientific and healthcare literature worldwide.

A colourful tribute to Isaac Elzevir, with the elm-tree emblem, adorns the Great Hall of the Library of Congress in Washington, DC.

Christopher Plantin's Polyglot Bible

Christopher Plantin (1514–89) began his career as a bookbinder in the French city of Caen in Normandy. In 1549 he settled in Antwerp and by the 1580s he was at the head of one of the most celebrated printing and publishing houses in Europe. Behind his logo of the golden compasses stood a large-scale industrial concern with an international clientele. He produced a wide range of literature, including liturgical books and hymnals, emblem books, pocket editions of Cicero, Aesop's *Fables* and an edition of Andreas Vesalius's *De humani corporis fabrica* with copper-plate anatomical engravings.

Publishing was a dangerous profession in the Spanish Netherlands. Printers who fell foul of the authorities could be imprisoned or executed. Plantin trod a fine line between conformity and illegality. Although he kept quiet about any Protestant sympathies he may have had, in 1561 the Spanish governor ordered his workshop searched for heretical works. Plantin solved the problem by selling his entire stock and repurchasing it later when the situation had calmed down. In 1563 he went into partnership with four Calvinists, who provided him with essential business capital. But when the Duke of Alva entered Brussels in 1567 to subdue the rebellious Netherlands at the orders of the Catholic king of Spain, executing thousands in the process, Plantin had to sever all relations with his Protestant partners in order to survive. Plantin knew that he now needed a powerful patron, and who better than Philip II, the king of Spain himself?

It was for Philip that Plantin produced his 'polyglot Bible', with parallel texts in Latin, Greek, Hebrew, Syriac and Aramaic. The project was first vetted by the Inquisition, an essential preliminary to winning the king's approval. It was an enormously expensive investment, and Plantin's entire business was mortgaged to the king during production. Plantin needed characters in all the languages in question: the French printer Garamond provided him with the steel punches from which he made the matrices. The polyglot Bible kept thirteen presses and fifty-five men occupied, not to mention the job of proofreading, which was done by several expert linguists as well as Plantin's own teenage daughter. It was said that she

The frontispiece to Plantin's polyglot Bible, produced in Antwerp in eight folio volumes between 1568 and 1572. Only a few copies survive; many were lost at sea on their way to Spain. The group of animals probably symbolized the unity of Christianity.

could correct the script perfectly accurately, but without understanding a word of it. The eight volumes were in folio format, so only two pages could be printed at a time. The task took four years, from 1568 to 1572, but it made Plantin a favoured subject of the Spanish crown. He earned the title of Proto-Typographer to the King, with a lucrative monopoly on the printing of liturgical works.

In 1581 the Netherlands declared independence from Spain. When William the Silent, the leader of the Dutch uprising, entered Antwerp, Plantin had to do another U-turn in favour of Dutch Protestantism, but without antagonizing the king of Spain. He managed to perform a successful balancing act, printing for the Dutch States-General, while maintaining subsidiaries both in Holland and in Paris, the centre of Counter-Reformation publishing. When he died in 1589, he left his son-in-law Jan Moretus (1543–1610) to continue his flourishing publishing dynasty.

Above: A double-page spread from Plantin's polyglot Bible. From left: the Hebrew text, its Latin translation, the Greek text, its own Latin translation, and underneath the Aramaic text on the left and its Latin translation on the right. The New Testament had versions in Greek and Syriac, each with Latin translations.

Left: The 'Golden Compasses' was the name of the building occupied by the Plantin–Moretus printing shop, here shown in Plantin's logo as drawn by Peter Paul Rubens.

The Inquisition and the Index

The rapid spread of the Protestant Reformation provoked a reaction from the papacy and from university theology faculties that had responsibility for censorship. Between 1544 and 1556, the Sorbonne in Paris issued 500 condemnations of heretical works; the University of Louvain Indexes published in 1546, 1550 and 1558 listed 700 prohibitions in total, while the Spanish Inquisition, which was always something of a law unto itself, identified even more. Censorship was a special concern of the Catholic Church, since it had always assumed the role of defining orthodox doctrine and defending it against heretical interpretations. The Index of Prohibited Books (*Index librorum prohibitorum*) identified the Church's blacklisted publications, and the list grew longer in the Counter-Reformation. By 1790, there were about 7,400 banned titles on the Index.

The Inquisition was established in Rome by Pope Paul III in 1542. It was essentially a court, answerable directly to the Pope himself, and so was often very unpopular with local bishops who had little control over its decisions. In 1558 the first Roman Index of Prohibited Books announced approximately a thousand prohibited titles, including the works of Erasmus, Machiavelli and Rabelais – a declaration of war on Europe's intellectual elite. In 1572 the Congregation of the Index was set up as a separate office with responsibility for keeping the blacklist up to date. Subsequent editions of the Index were more sophisticated: they graded authors according to their supposed degree of toxicity, and they marked specific passages for expurgation rather than condemning entire books. Erasmus, for one, was treated more leniently. The Inquisitors tried to ban the reading of religious books in the vernacular and even opposed the reading of romances, demonizing books to such an extent that just owning one was regarded as suspicious. One Venetian artisan was accused of heresy in 1572 simply because he had been caught reading books in a neighbour's house.

Repression could not be imposed effectively everywhere. Although Philip II of Spain established the Inquisition in three New World centres – Lima, Mexico City and Cartagena de Indias – implementation in the Americas was patchy because of its distance from Spain and the lack of qualified personnel. The Inquisition could not even cover the whole of Italy adequately, and its activities were more or less confined to the Alps and the northern parts of the country where the risk of Protestant infiltration was considered highest. In reality, repression was weak and episodic; in France the bans were consistently ignored.

The Congregation of the Index survived as an official institution until 1917, and the Vatican abolished the Index itself in 1966.

The frontispiece to a 1786 edition of the Index of Prohibited Books, showing books being burned. At the base is the citation from the Acts of the Apostles used to justify the practice. According to an old belief, 'good' books would float intact over the flames, while pernicious literature was reduced to ashes.

Mesoamerican Codices

The conquistadors brought their distinctive cultural baggage, in the form of books, from Spain to the New World. But they did not arrive in an illiterate society. Although the Incas had no great writing tradition, Mexico and Central America had rich literary cultures predating the Hispanic period, which missionaries and conquistadors tried – in vain – to destroy.

The books of the conquistadors were the books of the Counter-Reformation: missals, Bibles, books of hours, lives of the saints and theological works. About 70 per cent of all the books shipped from sixteenth-century Spain were ecclesiastical, and were intended to aid in the conversion of indigenous peoples to Catholicism. Zealous friars saw Mayan and Aztec books as works of the devil, and in a series of ecclesiastical pogroms many were destroyed. Although hundreds of indigenous books were in use in Mesoamerica before the Spanish conquest, only fifteen from that period now survive.

On the peninsula of Yucatán the conquistadors encountered the traditional written culture of the Maya, and in Mexico that of the Nahua, also known as the Aztecs. Mesoamericans wrote on paper derived from the inner bark of the wild fig tree. The Nahua called it *āmatl* and their word for the book itself – *amoxtli* – derived from this. The Maya knew it as *huun*. Mayan *huun* paper developed in the fifth century. It was much more durable than the papyrus used throughout the Mediterranean world. The material was coated with lime plaster, which created a smooth white surface for painting. Mesoamerican codices were often folded concertina-style into 'screenfold' books. When they were unfolded, the reader could view several pages at once.

In the Mayan writing system, each sign or glyph represented a creature, an idea or an object. Many glyphs are cryptic and open to different interpretations; scholars are still deciphering them, but it is apparent that Mayan script became increasingly phonetic over time. Over 800 characters have been identified, but many more exist: the Hieroglyphic Stairway at Copán in Honduras has about 1,300 glyphs carved in stone, recounting the deeds and genealogies of local leaders.

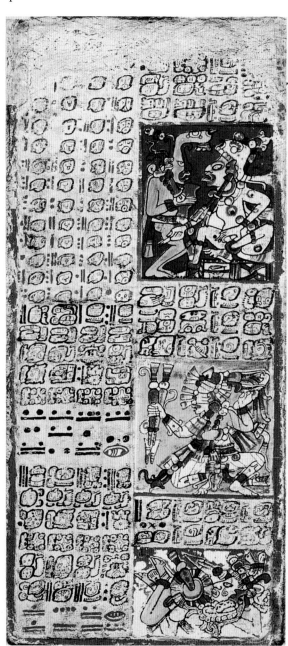

A leaf from the Dresden Codex, made from fig bark covered in a lime-based coating and inscribed on both sides. It was used for astronomical calculations and divination.

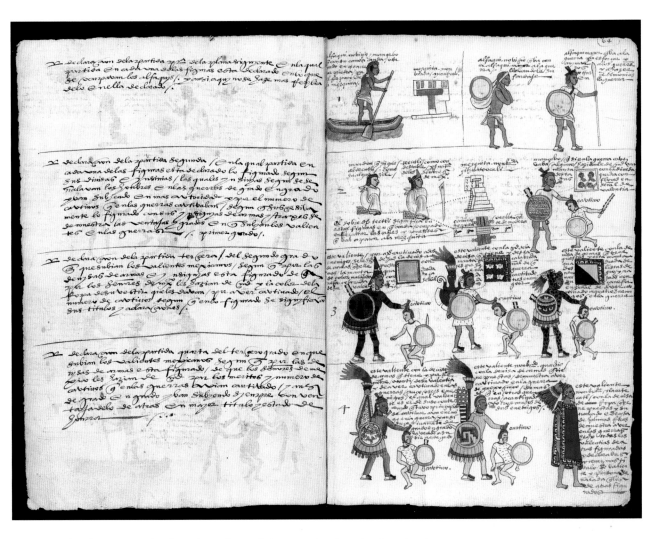

Mayan books were guides for priests about divinatory rituals, calendars, local histories and royal genealogies. They recorded hundreds of years of Maya history, the story of a civilization that flourished between the third and tenth centuries in the Yucatán peninsula and the Guatemalan highlands, recounting lives of rulers and dignitaries, and key events such as conquests. Calendar books functioned as sacred almanacs, carrying vital astrological information – for example, on the cycle of Venus, which was used to find propitious moments for war and coronations.

The Maya also had medical treatises, maps and books about plants and animals. The Dresden Codex survives in the state library of Dresden (there is an exact replica in the National Library in Guatemala City). This codex is made up of a single long sheet that is folded like an accordion to make thirty-nine leaves, written on both sides. It dates from the eleventh or twelfth century, making it the earliest surviving book from the Americas. It is thought to have been brought to Europe by conquistadors in the sixteenth century, and was purchased by the director of the Royal Library at Dresden in

The Codex Mendoza is a colonial Aztec book commissioned by the viceroy of New Spain and named after him. It was probably produced from 1541 to 1542, about twenty years after the Spanish conquest, on European paper with a Spanish commentary on the pictographs. This page explains the duties of novice priests (top) and the ranks of Aztec warriors (bottom).

1739 from a private collector in Vienna. It contains a number of divinatory Mayan texts, including astronomical tables and almanacs.

The Codex Mendoza is a Nahua book commissioned by the Spanish colonial authorities in 1541 as a gift for Charles V of Spain. It contains a history of the Aztec kings, records the tributes due to local rulers before the conquest, as well as to the Spanish afterwards, and gives ethnographic information on the everyday lives of the Aztecs. It also includes a commentary by a Spanish priest.

In Mexico, the screenfold books of the Nahua were made from tanned deer hides. Unlike Mayan codices, the books of the Aztecs were mainly pictorial. The arrival of Hernán Cortes's expedition, for example, was immediately recorded in paintings, which were taken to the Aztec ruler Montezuma to warn him. Another Aztec screenfold book, the Codex Borbonicus, was copied by Nahua priests shortly before or just after the Spanish conquest. It is made from a single folded sheet of *āmatl* paper nearly 15 metres (50 feet) long and contains a divinatory calendar, an outline of the Mesoamerican fifty-two-year cycle, and the series of rituals and ceremonies attached to this cycle.

Several hundred such books have survived from the sixteenth century, although some are only fragmentary and the condition of others has deteriorated so much that they are illegible. They provide a valuable reflection of the life and cultures of Mexico and Central America before and immediately after the arrival of the Spanish.

The Codex Borbonicus is a divinatory Aztec calendar. Each page shows the ruling deity for the period together with other gods and symbols for each day. The Codex has some notes in Spanish, so it is not clear whether it is Pre-hispanic or not.

Don Quixote

Don Quixote or, to give the novel its full translated title, *The Life and Deeds of the Ingenious Gentleman Don Quixote of La Mancha*, made its author Miguel de Cervantes Saavedra (1547–1616) the pre-eminent figure of Spanish literature. Like Shakespeare and Molière, who play similarly prominent roles in the literatures of Britain and France, Cervantes with his ridiculous but sympathetic hero was able to appeal to both a courtly and a peasant audience.

Cervantes was born into a modest surgeon's family in Alcalá de Henares. His peripatetic life reads like that of one of his fictional characters. At some point he fled Spain, possibly as a result of a duel, and entered the service of Cardinal Aquaviva in Rome. In 1570 he enlisted and served in the great naval battle of Lepanto against the Turks. He was then captured by North African pirates, and had to be ransomed. Eventually he settled in Madrid.

Below left: The title page of the first edition of *Don Quixote* from 1605, bearing a long dedication to the Duke of Bejar and the Latin motto *Spero lucem post tenebras* ('After darkness I seek the light').

Below right: Thomas Shelton's first complete English translation of *Don Quixote*, *The History of Don Quichote*, appeared in 1620 and was popular throughout the seventeenth century. The title page shows Don Quixote with his squire Sancho Panza and a windmill in the background, which became a well-known symbol of the story.

The publication of the first part of *Don Quixote* in 1605 made Cervantes famous. Several pirated editions appeared immediately. In 1614 a false second part appeared under the pen name of Avellaneda, a mysterious author who has never been satisfactorily identified. This hurried Cervantes into completing the genuine second part, which appeared in 1615, a year before his own death. By this time, Part One had already been translated into English, French and Italian and published in Lisbon, Milan and Brussels.

In chapter 62 of Part Two, the Don visits a printing-house in Barcelona, one of the curiosities of the city, and finds that what is being printed there is...Part Two of *Don Quixote*, by Cervantes's unidentified imitator. All the processes of book production – from typesetting to proof correction – are mentioned in this chapter, revealing an author painfully aware of how much of the production process had escaped his personal control. Not only did pirate editions of his work appear with impunity, but the process of textual revision and proof-reading that went on in the print-shop itself meant that, in 'golden age' Spain, the author could no longer supervise every transformation of his text.

An engraving from the luxury four-volume edition of *Don Quixote*, produced in 1780 by Joaquín Ibarra for the Royal Spanish Academy. No expense was spared; no longer merely a comic novel, the work had by then become part of the established literary canon.

Neither Cervantes nor his original publishers, the bookselling de Robles family, made much money out of *Don Quixote*. The first edition was produced in about 400 copies, but most of them were sent to the Americas, where bigger profits could potentially be made. Unfortunately, 1605 was a disastrous year for the galleon fleet, and most of the print run was lost in shipwrecks in the Caribbean. But seventy-two copies of the first edition did reach Peru in 1606. Foreign editions, abridged versions and unscrupulous imitations earned the author nothing.

In 1636–37, both parts of the novel were published at the Spanish court – a major step in the canonization of Cervantes – and several Madrid reprintings followed, as well as a Flemish series of illustrated editions, which was launched in 1662 in Brussels. After 1660, the book started to acquire a more popular readership. Cheap Spanish editions multiplied, using engraved illustrations borrowed from overseas versions, which often bore little relation to Spanish realities. Until the mid-eighteenth century, *Don Quixote* was usually produced in two-volume quarto editions on mediocre paper.

In the second half of the eighteenth century, the book's long publishing saga changed direction when a sumptuous edition was produced in England with a life of Cervantes attached. Joaquín Ibarra produced a four-volume Spanish luxury edition for the Royal Spanish Academy in 1780. During the Age of Enlightenment, Cervantes was read by both lower-class readers and the social elite.

Don Quixote has inspired many illustrators. The French caricaturist Honoré Daumier (1808–79) produced an extensive set of paintings and drawings that were shown at the Paris Salon of 1850. Gustave Doré produced a further collection of drawings in 1863, showing the Don being driven out of his mind by excessive reading of romances. Pablo Picasso followed suit almost a century later, and his pen-and-ink drawing has become the most widely recognized portrait of Don Quixote.

French caricaturist Honoré Daumier produced many drawings and paintings on the theme of Don Quixote, who fascinated him in the later years of his life. Like most of the artist's work, his portraits were simple and unflattering.

Ars moriendi: Books on How to Die

Ars moriendi, or 'The Art of Dying', was a staple genre of religious literature. Anonymous texts circulated widely in two major related versions, usually published in small-format books cheaply illustrated with woodcuts. About 50,000 copies were printed in the *incunabula* period before 1501. The genre was at its height in the late fifteenth and early sixteenth centuries: from then on, its popularity declined in favour

Demons torment the dying man in this illustration of *Ars moriendi*. One is holding up a list of sins, while others are present to collect debts owed to them.

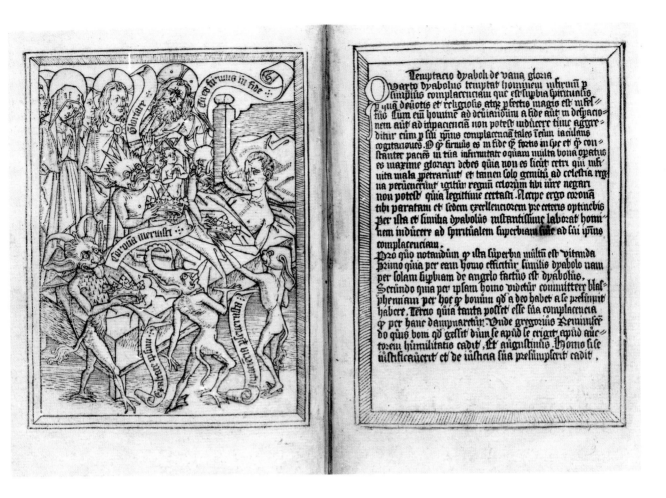

of Erasmus's treatise on preparing for death, *De preparatione ad mortem* (1534). The earliest versions were probably composed in southern Germany, but hundreds of manuscripts of *Ars moriendi* survive in several languages, along with a series of woodcuts that circulated both as printed books and as individual engravings that could be easily pinned to the wall.

In traditional versions, angels and demons competed for the soul of the dying person. The approaching Last Judgment, with its threats and torments intended to strike terror into the sinner's heart, was a favourite theme for illustrators. The macabre sensibility of this late medieval period generated gruesome images of corpses and prancing skeletons. The way to die well was to resist the five diabolical temptations: loss of faith, despair, impatience, pride and avarice. Christians were also urged, well before their demise, to make wills setting up charitable donations and investing in posthumous Masses to be spoken for their souls. On one's deathbed it was ideal to be surrounded by family and the clergy, to make a final confession and receive the sacrament. If all went well, the soul, sometimes depicted as a miniature person, would be carried up to heaven by angels. If not, the fires of hell or years in Purgatory awaited.

Devils tempt the dying man with crowns in this Dutch version from the 1460s; he must overcome the sin of pride to be saved. This 'block book' is made up of woodcuts, allowing text and image to be combined.

Emblem Books

The emblem book appeared in the sixteenth century and remained popular until the eighteenth century. It consisted of three main elements: firstly, an icon or image, for example, a plant, an animal or a statue; secondly, a motto; and thirdly, a text explaining the connection between image and motto. The texts varied from only a few lines in verse to several pages of prose. The notion was to draw out hidden meanings from the image and elucidate metaphors and associations that were not self-evident.

The first emblem book was published in Augsburg, written by the Milan lawyer Andrea Alciato (1492–1550). It contained about a hundred short verses in Latin on, for example, the lute, which represented the need for harmony rather than warfare in Italy's city-states, and the oak, whose strength reflected that of the Holy Roman Emperor Charles V. 'Silence' was depicted as a humanist working in his study. Writers of emblem books plundered examples from Greek and Roman sources, including Aesop's *Fables* and Plutarch's *Lives*. The texts were often crudely illustrated with woodcuts, but later were adorned with engravings. In Lyon publishers such as Bonhomme produced beautiful editions with decorative borders.

Andrea Alciato's enigmatic *Emblematum Liber* started the vogue for emblem books. The first unauthorized edition was published in Augsburg in 1531. The *Emblematum libellus* (Little Book of Emblems) shown here was produced later in Paris. On the left, a king squeezes a sponge as he extracts taxes from his subjects; the lioness on the right is a symbol of bravery.

The result was a new literary genre specializing in a repertoire of signs and symbols that could be reused by painters and architects. A scythe represented death, while the sword and scales represented justice. In fact, many of the pictorial elements discussed in emblem books were already part of the decor of everyday life, present on furniture and clothing, street signs and the façades of buildings.

Emblem books were descended from medieval bestiaries, which explained the symbolic importance of animals, and from proverbs and fables. They dealt with love, as in the Dutch *Emblemata amatoria* (1606) by Daniel Heinsius; religion, as in the French *Emblèmes, ou Devises chrétiennes* (1571) by Georgette de Montenay; and politics, as in the German *Emblemata politica* (1617) by Peter Isselburg. The Jesuits adopted the emblem book for didactic purposes, utilizing the hitherto profane genre to produce pious texts that read like sermons.

SI IAM ACCENSVS.

L'Euangile est comme feu estimé.
Car aussi tost que lon va le preschant,
Le monde en est tout soudain allumé.
Mais cela vient de la part du meschant.
Ce feu brulant, glaiue à double trenchant,
De tous costez viuement coupe & brule.
De l'vne part purge l'or & l'argent,
D'autre il consume & la paille & l'estule.

Above: Georgette de Montenay, who was probably a Calvinist, christianized the emblem book in her *Emblèmes, ou Devises chrétiennes*, published in French in Lyon around 1571. In this image, the world is set on fire by the Holy Gospel.

Left: In contrast, profane love was the subject of *Amorum emblemata*, illustrated here by Dutch courtier and painter Otto van Veen (Otto Vaenius) and published in Antwerp in 1608.

3 ENLIGHTENMENT AND THE MASSES

The eighteenth century was the French century. French, rather than Latin, became the common language of the educated classes all over the world, and the literature and ideas of the French Enlightenment had a broad international influence. This 'Age of Reason' was also an age of expanding book production. During the second half of the century, books became familiar consumer objects in Western Europe. Literacy rose markedly in the West after about 1750 and a large urban reading public emerged.

Publishers and printers had to contend with censorship and intrusive policing of their activities, especially in continental Europe, but found ingenious ways of getting their products into the hands of their customers. At the end of the eighteenth century, recreational fiction began to dominate the urban market in the West, pushing aside the legal tomes and religious works that had hitherto been at the centre of book production. Sentimental, scurrilous and so-called 'Gothic' novels, in which the British seemed to specialize, kept keen readers in eager anticipation all over Europe.

In the countryside, reading habits were more traditional. A plentiful chapbook literature fed the imagination of peasant readers, while catechisms and prayer books remained staple fare. But this idyllic literary world was shattered in 1789 when the French peasants and their urban compatriots took up arms in revolution. The apparatus of censorship, already dysfunctional, now crumbled away, leaving an unregulated market and a publishing world promising opportunity for the daring, and disaster for those who failed to adapt to the new logic of free enterprise.

A lithograph by an unknown artist, from the Musée Carnavalet, Paris, showing an early nineteenth-century book- and print seller and his well-dressed customers.

Literacy in the West

Literacy – the ability to read and write – had many faces in eighteenth- and nineteenth-century Europe. Some people could read print but not cursive handwriting, others could read the black Gothic script of their Bible but little else. Many learned to read in their youth, but lost the skill through lack of practice, and became illiterate again. According to official figures, increasing numbers of people in the West were gaining access to literacy after about 1750. Near-universal literacy was eventually achieved in Western Europe, Australia and the USA by the 1890s, when almost all the population could read and write. Only at that point did a genuine mass reading public exist, spurring the revolutionary expansion of the book trade.

Progress was fragile, inconsistent and uneven. In England, 60 per cent of men and 40 per cent of women were literate by 1800. By this time, almost all white men in New England were literate, but here literacy developed in a largely religious context, as there

A painting by François Vispre (1730–90) showing a gentleman reading the *Odes* of Horace in relaxed mode. The Latin classics were an integral part of the education of any eighteenth-century gentleman.

A reading scene by George Morland (1763–1804) entitled *Domestic Happiness*. It formed part of a narrative series of six paintings known as the 'Laetitia series'.

were few opportunities and little practical need for reading and writing in everyday society. On the eve of the French Revolution, half of the male population of France could read, and about 27 per cent of French women could do so. In eastern Europe, the proportion remained far lower until the literacy drives promoted by communist regimes in the twentieth century. In Lutheran Sweden and Finland, high literacy rates were achieved very early, by the eighteenth century, but Scandinavian literacy was largely confined to reading, usually limited to the Bible and the catechism. Swedes learned to write only much later, in the nineteenth century. Early modern Iceland was an exceptional case: Icelanders achieved widespread literacy without schools, libraries or printed books, learning to read and write via informal tuition by pastors and peasant teachers.

Literacy depended on social status and urbanization. Towns were always more literate than the countryside, and large cities more literate than small towns. Merchants, lawyers and aristocrats usually had literacy rates of 75 to 90 per cent in the seventeenth century, but to ordinary labourers literacy often seemed irrelevant, and perhaps only one in ten could read and write. Formal education did not play a decisive role in the growth of Western literacy: Britain and France, for example, achieved almost universal literacy in the nineteenth century, well before a system of free and compulsory primary schooling had been put in place. For centuries, ordinary people had become literate without ever attending school. They learned from family members, fellow workers or benevolent employers.

There was a persistent gap between male and female literacy rates. Many women were readers who never crossed the writing threshold: Shakespeare's daughter could not sign her own name, but that did not mean that she could not read. In most European societies women were taught to read the Bible and the catechism, but (like black slaves in the American South) they were not encouraged to learn to write, as writing conferred a certain independence that was considered a male prerogative. In the nineteenth century, job opportunities as teachers and shop assistants became increasingly available to women, creating new incentives to become fully literate. By 1900, female literacy rates in the West had officially caught up with those of men.

Despite the patchy progress in achieving widespread literacy in Europe, even the completely illiterate still had access to books. Like those who listened to political journals read aloud on Parisian street-corners during the French Revolution, there were many readers who 'heard' their books. Archbishop Ussher, who became Primate of All Ireland in the early seventeenth century, was taught to read by two aunts, both of whom had been blind from birth and had learned their scriptures by hearing them read aloud. In early modern Hungary, even people who could only sign their names with a mark still owned books, which literate friends and family members might read to them aloud.

The two young girls depicted here are Signe and Henriette, sisters of the Danish painter Constantin Hansen, painted in 1826. Sharing books was very popular among young middle-class women.

Evolution of the Printing Workshop

In the late eighteenth century, the book-manufacturing process had changed little since Gutenberg. Paper was still made from cloth gathered by ragpickers. Ink was commonly produced from a mixture of walnut husks, resin, linseed and turpentine. Type was typically composed of lead, which has a low melting point, and antimony, which hardens the lead. Typesetting was still done by hand, and the accuracy of any text was at risk if the printers had drunk too much beer with breakfast, or if the compositors were working in a hurry to meet a deadline. Competent proofreading was still a rarity.

Printers needed good light for typesetting, access to the sun for drying the sheets and a source of water for dampening the paper before printing. In London's cramped printing houses, the printers and compositors often occupied the upper storeys where there was more natural light. Storing paper was a problem and a perpetual fire hazard. Overturned candles and stacks of paper stored in an attic made a highly inflammable combination; print shops were vulnerable to sudden blazes, such as the one that gutted Samuel Richardson's shop in London in 1752.

Print-workers were paid according to the number of impressions they accomplished. The normal output was reckoned at 250 sheets per hour, or 2,500 impressions in the

Printers' guilds were a source of pride for members but tended to become exclusive. In this 1733 engraving of a guild tablet, a Regensburg printer celebrates his ancestry with a genealogical tree.

usual ten-hour working day. Although print-workers were relatively well paid, the supply of work varied erratically. In London there were slack periods in mid-winter and mid-summer, when two important customers – Parliament and the law courts – were in recess. Printers did not keep regular working hours: to get a task done, they might work on holidays, or not, as they themselves decided. They rarely had any savings, and in illness or old age they would be dependent on public charity.

Print-workers were a tightly knit and self-governing community. Like experts in any specialized trade, they had their own codes and jargon. The men who pulled the presses were the 'horses' ('bears' in France), the compositors were known as 'monkeys' and the boys who did menial jobs were the 'devils'. The workers belonged to a 'chapel', paying fines to the kitty for fighting, too much drinking and unruly behaviour.

The book trade was still ruled by a guild system. In London, the Stationers' Company was part of the pageantry of the City, parading on festive occasions in scarlet or blue-and-brown gowns, or sailing down the Thames in their ceremonial barge. In France, members of the guild (known as Le Corps or La Communauté de la Librairie et de l'Imprimerie) organized solemn Masses and banquets in commemoration of their patron-saint John the Evangelist, and held initiation ceremonies for new members. The French printers' guild was responsible for inspecting print shops to make sure standards were maintained and no contraband was slipping through customs. It was a privileged group, enjoying tax exemption from their sales of books.

In spite of such long-standing traditions, the book trade was evolving. By 1800, the guilds could no longer prevent upstart competitors from undercutting them. Cheap, unregulated labour undermined the hierarchy of skill and experience that had united master, journeyman and apprentice. After 1800, mechanization started to threaten jobs. The ancient corporate structure was cracking at the seams as the industry embarked on a painful period of modernization.

Habit d'Imprimeur en Lettres.

Above: A French satirical print by Nicolas de Larmessin from *c.* 1680, showing the 'costume of the printer of letters'. The essentials of the apparatus had not changed since the time of Gutenberg.

Left: A trade card for Thomas Kinnersby, bookseller, stationer and publisher at the paper-mill near St Paul's churchyard where much of the London book trade was concentrated in the eighteenth century. Presented in a decorative frame, the card advertised Kinnersby's address as well as the various wares he sold.

Censorship in the Age of Enlightenment

Has any system of censorship ever been effective? During the French Enlightenment, the *ancien régime* tried in vain to silence its critics and prevent the circulation of subversive works. It employed an army of censors, as well as inspectors who snooped around bookshops checking for illegal material. But even those in charge of the system recognized that every forbidden book would eventually find its way into print.

Although some celebrated authors certainly suffered from the repressive system, rough treatment at the hands of the law was often good publicity. Voltaire (1694–1778) was sentenced to two spells in the prison of the Bastille in 1711 and 1726, and the Paris Parlement (the supreme court) ordered the arrest of Jean-Jacques Rousseau (1712–78) after the publication of his *Émile* in 1762. But printers and booksellers suffered even more – in fact, they outnumbered authors by two to one in the Bastille. When the revolutionary crowd eventually stormed the Bastille on 14 July 1789, they found stacks

Printers were just as likely as authors to fall foul of censorship laws and have their presses seized. In this scene from the early nineteenth century, the offender is the printer of the French periodical *Le Temps*. Printers are being questioned and a clerk, seated at a table, is keeping a record of proceedings.

of banned books ready for pulping. The censorship system could not stem the rising tide of oppositional literature.

One problem for the monarchy was the ease with which French authors could publish controversial works in Switzerland, England or the Netherlands. Montesquieu's *De l'Esprit des lois* (On the Spirit of the Laws), for example, was published in Geneva in 1748. A book's imprint could never be completely trusted: Denis Diderot's *Pensées philosophiques* (1746) appeared anonymously with 'The Hague' on the title page, although it had actually been printed in Paris. Banning a book played into the hands of foreign competitors and hurt the French book trade, without actually preventing publication.

A second problem was the system's unwillingness to enforce its own repressive rules. Under Malesherbes's comparatively liberal direction of the French book trade (1750–63), many works received a 'tacit permit'. This meant that a publication was not authorized by the grant of a full royal *privilège*, but the government promised not to prosecute the author, printer or bookseller. The monarchy, in other words, agreed to turn a blind eye.

THE MAN WOTS GOT THE WHIP HAND OF 'EM ALL

The power of the free press is satirized in this engraving by Thomas MacLean from 1829, entitled 'The Man wots got the whip hand of 'em all'.

In reality, many authors were on very good terms with the regime. Voltaire himself was appointed Historiographer Royal and Gentleman of the Royal Bedchamber by Louis XV in 1745. A great patron could set up a writer for life, as Diderot found when the Russian empress Catherine II purchased his library and papers for 60,000 livres, thus wiping out all his debts and guaranteeing him a comfortable old age. If all else failed, an author could perhaps find a position as a royal censor. The job was unpaid, but there was a very good chance of a royal pension after twenty years' service. There were 178 censors on the eve of the Revolution, including eminent literary figures such as the philosopher Étienne Bonnot de Condillac.

Under Napoleon, book production in the French Empire once again became strictly regulated by the state. In 1811 the number of printers in Paris was limited to eighty; they were strictly licensed, and only four newspapers were allowed to appear. All new books had to be registered and approved before printing. The fewer printers and newspapers there were, the easier it was for the regime to maintain surveillance over what was published.

Forbidden Books

Banned books were sought after in France, but expensive. The well-heeled Parisian bourgeois Edmond-Jean-François Barbier (1689–1771) recorded his frustration in his diary when François-Vincent Toussaint's *Les Moeurs* was officially banned in 1748: he knew he would now have to pay double the normal price to get hold of a copy.

An elaborate clandestine network ensured that contraband books and pornography travelled from Swiss publishing centres to reach readers in France. Mule-drivers took consignments over the Jura mountains to a merchant on the other side of the border. The merchant would bribe the customs agents and transport the forbidden books to a depot somewhere in the French provinces, perhaps Troyes or Lyon. From there they would be sold to disreputable provincial booksellers, or smuggled in small quantities to the main centres of consumption. There was no better secret route than in the baggage of a great aristocrat, which would never be searched. In this way, members of the court of Versailles iactively played a role in the secret chain that delivered banned books to Paris. Palms had to be greased, and banned books passed through so many hands between Switzerland and Versailles that their price inevitably rose by about 25 per cent, and would double again in Paris itself. The Baron d'Holbach's *Le Système de la nature* (1770) originally had a retail price of 4 livres, but its price in Paris was 10 livres. The clandestine book trade was an entire parallel industry operating very profitably alongside the legal production and sale of books.

Voltaire was among the top ten bestselling authors of banned works, but this rogues' gallery was also full of lesser-known and now forgotten writers. There was always a ready market in pre-Revolution Paris for caricatures and broadsheets that ridiculed the degenerate court, the king's sexual impotence, and Marie Antoinette's alleged bisexual practices. The regime tried but failed to limit the circulation of these libels (*chroniques scandaleuses*), which mixed political satire with outright pornography. The gutter press, as well as the intellectual elite, undermined the credibility of divine-right monarchy.

'The Austrian hen' was how this French etching satirized Marie Antoinette in 1791. The caption reads 'Gold and silver slide down with ease, but I cannot swallow the constitution'. The French Revolution led to an explosion of pamphleteering.

LA POULLE   D'AUTRȳCHE,

Je digere l'or l'argent avec facilitée|mais la constitution je ne puis l'avaler

Making a Profit

The production budget for the Baron d'Holbach's *Le Système de la nature* (1770), produced in Neuchâtel (Switzerland) at the end of the *ancien régime*, shows the enormous cost of paper at this time. For a volume in-octavo, with a print run of 1,670 copies, paper took up 63 per cent of the budget. Composition absorbed about 16 per cent and printing costs about 20 per cent. And yet, if the volume could be sold out for a retail price of 4 livres, the publisher could realize a profit of 170 per cent. No wonder that eighteenth-century readers were very sensitive to the quality of the paper in the books they bought: there was an enormous financial incentive for the publisher to substitute poor paper for fine.

French publishers did not pay authors on a royalty basis, that is to say, according to the number of copies sold. Instead they bought a manuscript for a lump sum. Jean-Jacques Rousseau sold what became his bestselling novel *La Nouvelle Héloïse* for only 2,160 livres to the Amsterdam publisher Rey who produced the first edition in 1764. He earned nothing from subsequent editions, and overall made even less from his *Du Contrat social* (1762), also sold to Rey. Without a royalty system and adequate copyright law, writers could not get rich from literary work alone.

Publishers themselves did not expect to make a large profit on a first edition. They banked on successful re-editions, whose sales would amortize all of their initial investment. Individual print-runs were therefore relatively small, and new novels

In this illustration from 1889 three women read the three successive volumes of a novel, possibly borrowed from a circulating library: the tranquil opening volume, the second with its awful disclosures and the third with the tearful dénouement.

rarely appeared in runs of more than 1,000 copies.

Reading rooms, or *cabinets de lecture*, establishments where for a small fee readers could hire a book by the hour, were precursors of modern libraries and an important and reliable market for books. Publishers seized on this opportunity by stretching out popular novels into three volumes, which enabled the reading rooms to hire out different volumes of the same title to multiple customers at once. This was the origin of the 'three-decker' novel. The three-volume system gave publishers a regular income, but kept the price of books artificially high. In Britain, for instance, the three-decker novel pushed up the price of novels by 300 per cent between the 1790s and 1840.

A prospectus for a book to be sold by subscription. This method allowed the publisher to test the market in advance and, in the case of expensive works, to collect a deposit to finance production.

Selling books by advance subscription presented several advantages to a prudent publisher. The pre-publication search for subscribers was a preliminary test of the market. If few subscribers came forward, the whole project could be abandoned without loss. If a suitable number declared an interest, production could go ahead in the clear knowledge of how many copies were needed to be profitable. This system also enabled the publisher to sell directly to interested customers without the need for a bookseller. Since subscribers paid their subscription volume by volume, a publisher with little working capital was guaranteed some income as more volumes were printed. If the plan did not work out, or funds ran short, the publisher might simply abandon production, leaving subscribers high and dry. In the 1820s and 1830s there were many disgruntled subscribers with incomplete editions of Voltaire's works on their shelves.

Eighteenth-century books were expensive. When Lord Byron's *Childe Harold's Pilgrimage* was published in 1812, a bound copy would have been completely unaffordable to a skilled craftsman, taken a large chunk out of a clergyman's annual income and cost a serving maid six weeks' wages. Even William Wordsworth, who had a respectable income from his government job as Distributor of Stamps for Westmorland, would have had some difficulty buying his own books.

In the early decades of the nineteenth century, print runs expanded with the invention of stereotyping. Previously, moveable type had to be reset for every new edition, but with stereotyping each sheet of type was fixed and preserved as a metal plate, which could be endlessly reused to produce reprints of the original edition. Publishers

An eighteenth-century Dutch bookshop, with a bookbinder working on the premises, engraved by Reinier Vinkeles (1741–1816). Books at the time were often sold unbound, leaving the customer to choose a personalized binding.

therefore found it more profitable than ever before to issue frequent reprints of a successful title. The same reprinted text could be bound in different ways to appeal to different markets, and the stereotyped plates themselves could be sold or hired out to other printers.

Stereotyping created substantial profit incentives for reprinting many old and obsolete titles. In London, a virtual cartel of publishers produced and reproduced old titles for the cheap end of the market. As a result, ordinary readers were fed not the exciting romantic writers who were at the cutting edge of literature, but the 'old canon' of Chaucer, Milton, Pope, Spenser, Defoe and Goldsmith. This created a two-tier book market. Wealthy readers demanded new, more expensive works, but less well-off readers were sold cheap reprints of uncontroversial pre-Enlightenment worthies.

Diderot's *Encyclopédie*

The *Encyclopédie*, usually associated with Denis Diderot (1713–84) and Jean d'Alembert (1717–83), was one of the major publishing operations of the eighteenth century. For more than twenty years it kept thousands of authors, printers and compositors in business. It was published from 1751 in seventeen folio volumes, followed by eleven more sumptuous volumes of engravings. The writing process engaged 150 of Europe's best intellectuals. Jean-Jacques Rousseau contributed about 400 articles, many of them on music, for which he received no payment; Voltaire wrote over forty, while Diderot himself wrote over 5,000 articles and made a significant contribution to the coverage of philosophy and the descriptions of arts and manufactures.

The *Encyclopédie* was more than just an encyclopaedia: it was a manifesto for the rational thinking and social criticism of the Age of Enlightenment. It aimed to disseminate up-to-date knowledge of scientific inventions and the practical arts, making new ideas and procedures accessible to any educated reader. The *Encyclopédie* also attacked prejudice and tradition, and put social and political institutions under the microscope, promoting liberal economic policies and an end to royal monopolies. It questioned the historical truth of the Bible, the reality of miracles and the Resurrection, and the principle of priestly celibacy. It attacked the parasitical position of the aristocracy, and defended individual property rights as the foundation of society. In 1752, after the publication of the second volume, the monarchy banned it, but this did not deter the editors, who continued the project with the tacit approval of figures close to the crown, such as Madame de Pompadour.

This portrait of French writer Denis Diderot was completed by Louis-Michel van Loo in 1767. Diderot's self-assured pose belies the exhausting labour he undertook to produce his *Encyclopédie* – a monument to the French Enlightenment.

In the first twenty years of its life, the folio *Encyclopédie* sold over 4,000 copies, and produced 2 million livres in profit. This was remarkable enough for a work of such size, but the appearance of ever cheaper editions in progressively smaller formats made the work even more accessible to the educated European public. Between 1777 and 1779, a quarto edition appeared in Switzerland in thirty-six volumes, with the subscription price reduced by more than half, to 384 livres. The Lausanne and Bern octavo edition of 1778–82 in thirty-nine volumes did away with most of the expensive engravings that had distinguished the original production, and used second-grade paper. It was assembled in a hurry, and readers would later complain that they found thumbprints on the pages and that there were many typographical errors. No matter, the cost had been reduced to only 225 livres, less than a quarter of the price of the folio edition.

Taking all of the eighteenth-century editions together, Diderot's *Encyclopédie* sold about 25,000 copies and reached the educated middle class in every urban centre of Europe. Copies were purchased by

Above: The Marquise de Pompadour (1721–1764), for a time Louis XV's favourite mistress, was a great supporter of Enlightenment intellectuals. In this painting by Maurice Quentin de La Tour, she is posing with a prospectus and several volumes of the *Encyclopédie*.

Left: The first edition of the *Encyclopédie*. The first of seventeen folio volumes appeared in 1751, accompanied by superb engravings. Later editions abandoned the engravings and adopted smaller formats to reach a wider audience across Europe.

members of the French clergy and the nobility – the very social groups whose privileged status would be destroyed by the Revolution. It sold well in the Netherlands and the Rhineland. In Italy, the Lucca folio edition of 1758–76 sold about 3,000 copies, while a subsequent Livorno edition sold another 1,500, printed under the patronage of Leopold, Duke of Tuscany, which effectively neutralized the Pope's hostility towards the project. The *Encyclopédie* had become a bestseller on a European scale.

Illustrations of printing processes and typefaces in the first edition of the *Encyclopédie*.

The Art of the Book

By the late eighteenth century, the market for books was booming across many literary genres. Elegant, well-crafted editions of classic works appeared alongside the entertaining fiction that was increasingly in demand. Publishers began to favour streamlined designs rather than the ostentatious decorations of baroque art. New and clearer typefaces were designed and lettering became more rounded and vertical; notes fell into disfavour, leaving more space for wide margins.

At the forefront of these new typographic designs was John Baskerville (1706–75), an English printer and varnisher. His varnishing business yielded enough profit to allow him to pursue his passions for type founding, ink manufacture and paper-making, drawing on his early training as a writing-master and headstone-engraver. Starting in 1750, he designed a new font that was more sober than its predecessors – particularly the fonts of William Caslon (1692–1766) – and had a stronger contrast between thick and thin strokes. He also found ways to enhance the opacity of ink and improve its drying capacity. In collaboration with the paper-maker James Whatman, he developed a process

John Baskerville's quarto edition of Virgil's *Aeneid*, printed in Birmingham in 1757. Baskerville developed darker ink and a sharply defined typeface to produce high-contrast texts with generous margins.

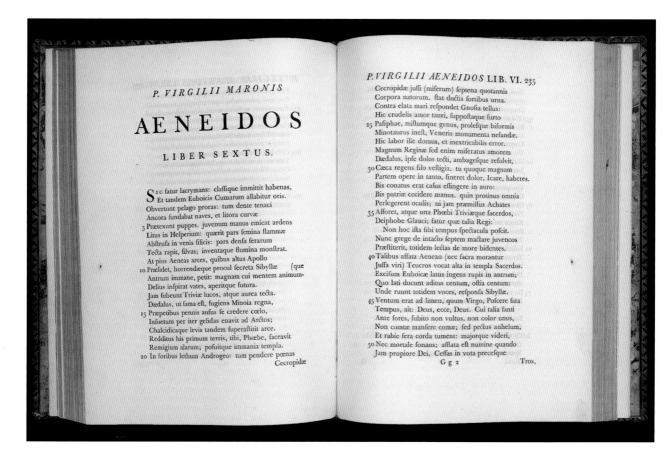

of producing perfectly smooth paper, using a fine wire mesh that left no lines from the mould on the page. 'Wove paper' was born.

In 1757 Baskerville published a remarkable quarto edition of Virgil on wove paper, using his own type. It took three years to complete, but it made such an impact that Baskerville was appointed printer to the University of Cambridge in 1758. Under the university's patronage he produced his masterpiece – a folio Bible – in 1763. But fellow printers criticized the severity of his design and the lustrous finish of his paper. Moreover, the books he created were expensive and only a few collectors were able to buy them. Baskerville died in poverty, relatively unappreciated in England, but his innovations influenced other European printers, such as the Didot family.

The first member of the Didot dynasty to achieve fame was François Didot (1689–1757), who in 1713 opened the bookshop *À la Bible d'or* (The Golden Bible) on the Quai des Grands-Augustins on the Left Bank in Paris. His son, François-Ambroise Didot (1730–1804), improved the single-action press and perfected wove paper, which was called *papier vélin* in France. (The story goes that it was Benjamin Franklin, himself a former printer, who first introduced English wove paper to the French book trade during his tenure in Paris as the first United States ambassador to France.) François-Ambroise made his own typefaces and defined the Didot point system for measuring fonts, which is still in use today. With the patronage of the Count of Artois, the younger brother of King Louis XVI, he produced a sixty-four-volume collection of French novels, as well as a monumental series of French classics destined for the education of the young Dauphin (the heir to the throne). François-Ambroise's son Pierre (1760–1853) received a gold medal at the 1798 industrial exhibition for an edition of Virgil, and was given an

This edition of Horace's *Odes* was the product of two descendants of the Didot printing dynasty in France: Pierre Didot printed the work using type designed and produced by his brother Firmin. They were rewarded by the French government in 1798.

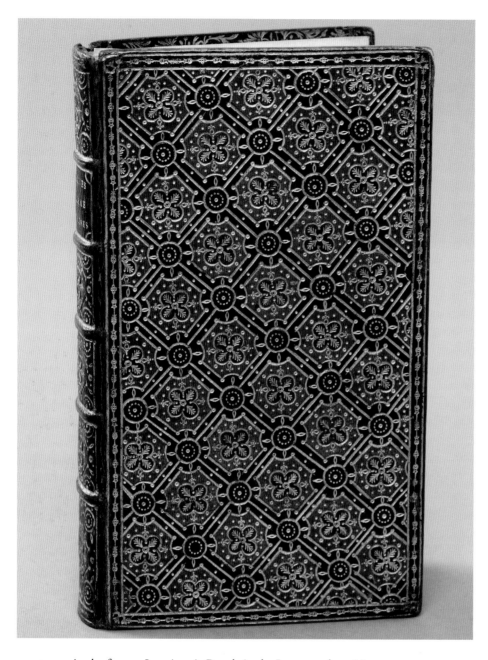

Nicolas Denis Derome, called 'Le Jeune', produced graceful decorative bindings in his innovative lacework style.

apartment in the former Imprimerie Royale in the Louvre palace. He went on to produce magnificent illustrated editions of Horace and Racine, using fonts designed by yet another Didot – his brother Firmin (1764–1836).

New styles of bookbinding appeared in this period. The 'mosaic' style, made up of different coloured leathers, was extremely popular, while in the *dentelle* ('lacework') style, the borders of the binding were decorated with foliage motifs. After Napoleon's expedition to Egypt in 1798, these designs gave way to a new vogue for neoclassical and Egyptian-inspired motifs.

Roman versus Gothic Type

During the Renaissance, simple and elegant typefaces based on Roman precedents were introduced, among them Claude Garamond's *gros romain*, designed in 1543, and the 'Cicero' font used by Robert Estienne. The descendants of these Renaissance fonts are still with us: our word-processors know them as Times New Roman (adapted from a sixteenth-century roman font developed by Robert Granjon, a colleague of Christopher Plantin), Antiqua (based on Aldus Manutius's roman font) or Garamond (adapted from Garamond's *gros romain*). However, Gothic script remained the popular choice for centuries, especially in the German-speaking and Nordic regions of Europe. When Martin Luther wanted his pamphlets to have a wide popular readership, he had them set in Gothic type. The choice between Gothic and roman depended on the nature of the text and the social status of its desired audience.

The flowing, Roman-style type of Claude Garamond was adopted by the French court in the 1540s and its influence spread to the rest of Europe. Garamond was probably influenced by the designs of the Venetian printer Aldus Manutius.

In Swedish book production, for example, Gothic type was overwhelmingly used for religious literature until the nineteenth century. Swedish printers had used Gothic print ever since printing began, although if a text quoted French or English citations, these would be rendered in roman. Gothic and roman script often defined quite different reading communities and social classes. For lower-class readers, chapbooks would be printed in Gothic. On the other hand, bourgeois readers of fiction, biography and the sciences preferred roman type. When the Royal Swedish Academy was established in 1739, all proceedings were ordered to be printed in roman script to meet the expectations of the international scientific community. Two Swedish book production systems therefore existed in parallel: one producing works primarily in Gothic, and one working exclusively in roman, depending on the markets for which they catered. Only in the course of the nineteenth century did roman replace Gothic type in Sweden, and the transformation was led by the educational system. In the Elementary School Reader of 1878, only 5 per cent of the text was still in Gothic.

Below left: The title page for a mid-eighteenth-century Swedish edition of Carl Linnaeus's *System of Nature*. Roman type was preferred to Gothic for the circulation of scientific work.

Below right: Gothic script, popular in German-speaking countries, was used for this first edition of Erich Maria Remarque's *Im Westen Nichts Neues*, translated in 1930 by Arthur Wesley Wheen who gave it its memorable English title, *All Quiet on the Western Front*.

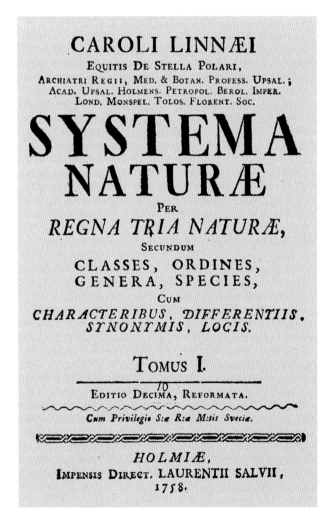

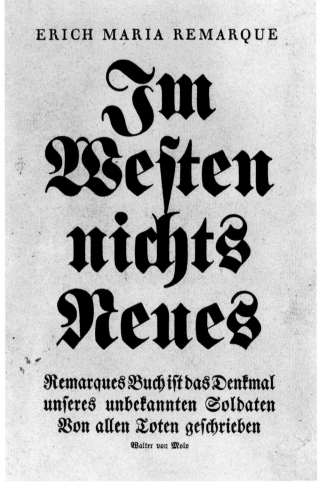

« Le Monde
Economie »

**G20 : comment sortir
de la guerre économique**
Supplément

Le Monde

Mardi 9 novembre 2010 · 66ᵉ année · N°20464 · 1,40 € · France métropolitaine · www.lemonde.fr —   Fondateur : Hubert Beuve-Méry · Directeur : Éric Fottorino

La grande distribution prédit le retour de l'inflation

« Un train de hausses de prix très importantes nous est présenté », explique au « Monde » Michel-Edouard Leclerc, dont l'enseigne détient 17,1 % de parts de marché en France
Il récuse l'argument des fournisseurs : la flambée des cours des matières premières

Bataille du rail autour d'un convoi nucléaire
Profitant du débat, les Verts allemands pourraient remporter le Land de Berlin. Page 4

Près de Laitzstelle, des antinucléaires allemands tentent de bloquer le convoi de déchets en provenance de France, dimanche 7 novembre.

The masthead for the prestigious French daily *Le Monde* uses Gothic type to suggest a long and distinguished tradition.

In Germany the battle between traditional Gothic and modern roman script continued during the first half of the twentieth century. The matter was even debated in the Reichstag before the First World War, but no conclusive decision was reached. The question of German national identity was at stake. The German book trade knew these two competing styles as Fraktur (Gothic) and Antiqua (roman). The Bauhaus school of art and design advocated Antiqua as a sign of modernity, just as Renaissance intellectuals had looked to ancient Rome for inspiration. For them, Fraktur isolated Germany from the international intellectual community. The traditionalists favoured Fraktur as an authentically 'German' font, as it had been used for the earliest vernacular texts in the early modern period, and they considered its thick black characters easier to read.

In 1928, 57 per cent of books published in Germany were in Fraktur. Even the first edition of Erich Maria Remarque's *All Quiet on the Western Front* (*Im Westen Nichts Neues*, 1929) came out in Fraktur. Then, in 1933, the Third Reich decreed that Fraktur was to be the national typeface used in all government publications, including school textbooks; in the same year, the Nazis closed the Bauhaus. But in 1941 there was a surprising about-face when the Reich Chancellery decided that Fraktur was based on characters introduced by Jewish newspaper owners and therefore had to be eliminated as a form of non-German contamination. After a brief revival following the Second World War, Fraktur gradually disappeared in Germany.

Gothic script is still with us, as a decorative font style conveying prestige, solemnity and age. It is often found in the mastheads of newspapers such as *The Washington Post*, *Le Monde* or *The Sydney Morning Herald*, a practice inherited from the earliest newspapers, which emerged when Gothic was still a standard display font. Universities use Gothic script in diplomas as a symbol of tradition, signalling their descent from medieval universities.

The Struggle for Copyright

It was in England and Scotland that authors first enjoyed a modern form of copyright, that is to say, some degree of ownership over the intellectual property they had created. The sums earned by British writers in the eighteenth century were the envy of Europe. Intellectual property was established only after long struggles in the courts, as publishers strenuously defended their traditional positions.

The Statute of Anne, which came into force in 1710 in England and Scotland, first recognized the author's (rather than the publisher's) right to intellectual property, and deemed that this right came into being with the act of composition. The 1710 law limited the publisher's exclusive copyright of a new book to fourteen years, renewable for a maximum of another fourteen years. For books already in print, exclusive copyright extended to twenty-one years. To introduce a law was one thing; to change deeply entrenched publishing practices was quite another, and the 1710 copyright law was not fully confirmed until it was tested in court. In 1774 the House of Lords, acting as Britain's supreme court of appeal, upheld a decision of the Edinburgh Court of Session in the case of Donaldson *vs.* Beckett, confirming that the perpetual copyright previously enjoyed by publishers was illegal. Following this ruling, a substantial amount of material entered the public domain. Older texts were available to be printed by anyone, and the protectionist guild mentality that had governed the world of London publishers became obsolete. Although the publishing industry responded by driving up the price of new books, the floodgates were opened to cheaper reprints, larger print runs, and a proliferation of anthologies and abridgements. The total yearly output of the British book trade increased four times over in the last quarter of the eighteenth century. Within five years of deregulation, Daniel Defoe's *Robinson Crusoe* sold more copies than it had done in the sixty years since its first publication in 1719.

The Copyright Act of 1814 went much further than the Statute of Anne, giving the author, rather than the publisher, the sole right to print a work for twenty-eight years after the first publication; in 1842 the author's copyright was extended to the author's lifetime plus seven years, or forty-two years after the date of first publication. There was, however,

The frontispiece of Daniel Defoe's *The Life and Strange Surprizing Adventures of Robinson Crusoe of York, Mariner*, which was internationally successful. It was frequently translated, imitated and abbreviated for educational purposes.

no reason why other countries should recognize British copyright laws, and publishers in the USA were free to reprint bestselling English works without any regard for their authors' intellectual property rights. For a time, much European literature was more freely available to American readers than it was to the European public. The British, of course, could reciprocate, and did so by producing their own offshore publications of American masterpieces such as Harriet Beecher Stowe's *Uncle Tom's Cabin* and the poetry of Henry Wadsworth Longfellow. The USA did not sign any international copyright agreement until 1891. In the international sphere, anarchy still reigned, and authors had no protection against piracy or plagiarism until the Bern International Copyright Convention of 1886 began to be enforced.

AN AUTHOR & BOOKSELLER

In this hand-coloured engraving by British humorist Thomas Rowlandson, a writer has some difficulty in persuading a bookseller to accept his manuscript. The bookseller appears to be a well-fed gentleman, in contrast to the author who is in need of a square meal.

The Pilgrim's Progress across the World

The Pilgrim's Progress, an allegorical novel by John Bunyan (1628–88), was the best-known text of all Protestant religions. For non-conformist Protestants, it was second in importance only to the Bible. First published in two parts in 1678 and 1684, it originally belonged to the radical Dissenting tradition of the seventeenth century. In the nineteenth century *The Pilgrim's Progress* became a transatlantic and an African bestseller. It conquered the world before 'returning' to England at the end of the nineteenth century to be incorporated belatedly into the English literary canon.

The Pilgrim's Progress tells the story of the trials of its hero, Christian, who struggles against temptation, despair and other hazards. He sheds his heavy burden of sin to arrive eventually at the celestial city, where he is united with God. The theology of the allegory was comprehensible and easily illustrated. The book functioned as a kind of surrogate Bible and was a useful Christian pedagogical tool, particularly in encouraging conversion; missionaries often bound it in with parts of the Bible. Some Africans therefore regarded the book as a white man's fetish with magical powers: in the 1830s, for example, Madagascans wanted a copy even if they were unable to read it.

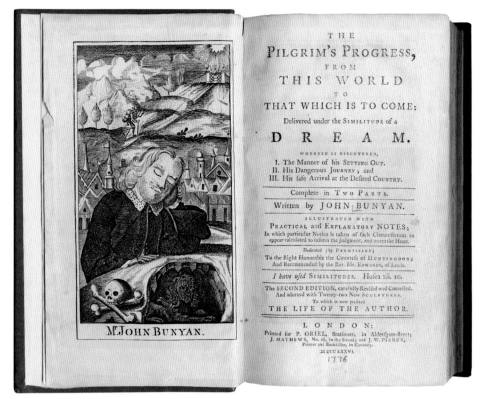

In this 1776 London edition of John Bunyan's *The Pilgrim's Progress* the author is shown asleep, dreaming of the landscape of temptation which his hero Christian will negotiate. This work did more than any other book, apart from the Bible, to popularize the teachings of Christianity.

A black Christian sets out in an African adaptation of *The Pilgrim's Progress*, sponsored by the London Missionary Society. Bunyan's novel had many different global incarnations.

The Pilgrim's Progress has been translated into 200 languages. It appeared in Dutch in 1681, in German in 1703 and in Swedish in 1727. The first North American edition was issued in 1681. During the colonial period, it was translated into over eighty different languages in Africa, where it helped to define the British empire as a single cultural space. In addition, there were twenty-four translations in South Asia, nine in South-east Asia and another eleven in Australasia and the Pacific.

Translations of Bunyan into non-European languages were the result of complex negotiations between missionaries and young converts, who were sometimes known as 'language boys'. The literal meaning of the text was not always easily translatable into African cultural contexts. For example, Kele Protestants in the Congo omitted the sections that explained the Christian concept of original sin, as this idea was incompatible with their cultural assumptions. The story was also changed in other ways to make it relevant to non-European audiences. African versions acquired black

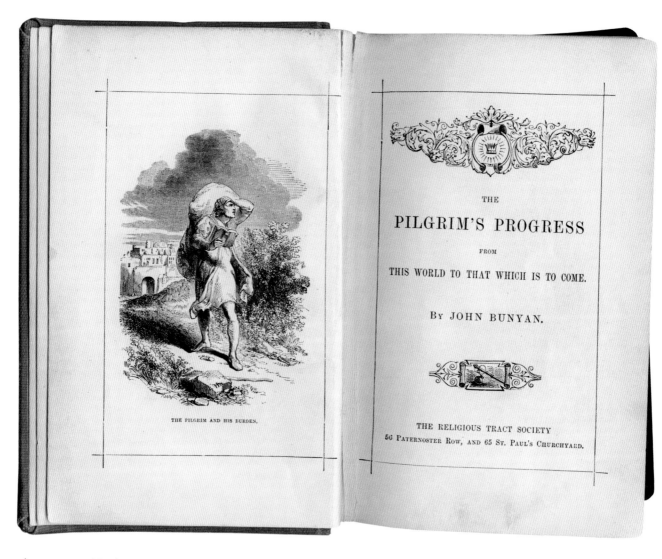

THE

PILGRIM'S PROGRESS

FROM

THIS WORLD TO THAT WHICH IS TO COME.

BY JOHN BUNYAN.

THE RELIGIOUS TRACT SOCIETY
56 PATERNOSTER ROW, AND 65 ST. PAUL'S CHURCHYARD.

THE PILGRIM AND HIS BURDEN.

characters, and in the East Cape, the African elite used *The Pilgrim's Progress* as a metaphor for their own struggle against apartheid. In the black Baptist culture of the American South, Bunyan's Christian became a black hero who was redeemed not only from sin but also from slavery.

In the English-speaking world, the book was often divided up into individual episodes, and transformed into postcards, wall-charts, sermons or magic lantern shows. During the late nineteenth and early twentieth centuries, the Religious Tract Society produced *The Pilgrim's Progress* in penny parts, Sunday School prize editions and cheap abridgements. There were Bunyan jigsaw puzzles, and some devoted followers even landscaped their gardens into Bunyan theme parks.

Bunyan's transnational hit had many uses and interpretations in different parts of the globe. Only in the early twentieth century was he fully recognized in his native country. In 1912 a stained-glass window in his honour was installed in Westminster Abbey.

A Religious Tract Society edition of *The Pilgrim's Progress.* **Founded in 1799, the society was a large-scale publisher of Christian books as well as pamphlets, targeting especially a young readership.**

Chapbooks

Chapbooks were cheap, anonymous publications that were the usual reading material for lower-class people who could not afford books. Members of the upper classes occasionally owned chapbooks, perhaps bound in leather with a personal monogram: the diarist Samuel Pepys had a specially bound collection of over 200. But printers typically tailored their texts for the popular market. Chapbooks were usually between four and twenty-four pages long, and produced on rough paper with crude, frequently recycled, woodcut illustrations. They sold in the millions.

In France, chapbooks were known collectively as the *bibliothèque bleue*, or 'blue library', because they were often wrapped in the cheap blue paper used as wrapping for sugar. In Spain, *pliegos sueltos* were literally 'loose sheets', folded once or twice over to make a booklet in quarto format. They were typically sold by itinerant peddlers, such as the *Jahrmarktströdler* in Germany and the *leggendaio* of sixteenth-century Italy. In seventeenth-century England, the production of chapbooks was controlled by a small group known as the Ballad Partners, who specialized in cheap items costing under 4d. In France, the 'blue library' made the fortunes of specialist publishers such as Oudot in

Below left: An anonymous French painting from 1623 of an itinerant bookseller (*colporteur*) in Paris, selling cheap brochures and pamphlets and crying his wares to the passing public.

Below right: The Spanish 'Romance of the Trojan Queen', dating from *c*. 1530, is an example of the cheap loose-sheet brochures known as *pliegos sueltos*, made up of a few folded pages, which were peddled by travelling salesmen.

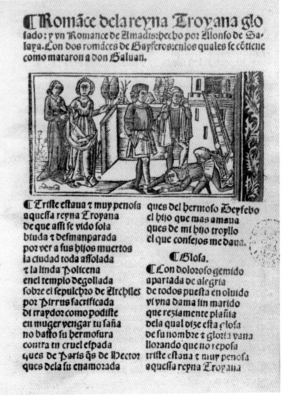

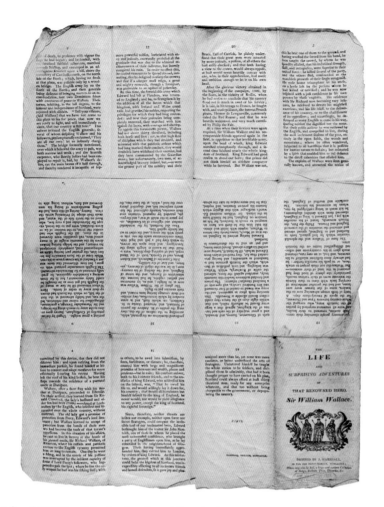

A Scottish chapbook of twelve pages, printed in Newcastle and relating 'The Life and Surprising Adventures of that Renowned Hero, Sir William Wallace'. Millions of such works were sold for popular consumption in Europe and became part of folk culture.

Troyes. After 1696 English chapbook peddlers had to be licensed, and 2,500 of them were then authorized, 500 in London alone. In France, there were 3,500 licensed *colporteurs* by 1848, and they sold 40 million books annually.

The chapbook repertoire was very stable, and its main components were constantly reissued. There were pious works, including catechisms, prayers, lives of the saints, homilies on the art of dying and versions of the *Danse macabre*. Peddlers also sold fiction, farces, burlesques and drinking songs. The chapbook corpus included myths, fairy tales, histories and romances: tales of Gargantua, Scaramouche and Tom Thumb; stories of great outlaws, usually glorifying their daring exploits against the rich; and chivalrous tales such as the story of Robert the Devil. Other titles offered solutions to problems of daily life: calendars, horoscopes, recipes, magical remedies and medical advice, instructions for card and dice games, etiquette books, alphabets for children and works of homely philosophy. Learned works were condensed, simplified and produced in short, easily digestible paragraphs for mass consumption, with blasphemous and obscene passages eliminated. Today much of this literature would be considered more suitable for children than for adults.

Almanacs

Almanacs were early reference books that functioned as annual diaries. They contained astrological tables, predictions and prophecies, and the dates of religious holidays, important fairs and the sittings of law courts. More than simply calendars, almanacs also provided an enormous amount of practical information, especially for farmers, including weather forecasts and sowing advice, along with recipes for cookery and herbal medicine.

Almanac production was probably at its height in the seventeenth century. In England, for instance, 460,000 copies of thirty different almanac titles were produced in 1687. The Stationers' Company defended its very lucrative monopoly on almanacs until the market was deregulated in 1775. In Germany, the *Badische Landeskalender* was produced in runs of 20,000 at the end of the eighteenth century, while 353,000 copies of *Vox Stellarum* appeared in London in 1800. Perhaps a quarter of a million almanacs were produced annually in late eighteenth-century Italy.

The *Grand Calendrier et compost des bergers*, published from 1491 until the end of the seventeenth century, was enormously successful not only in France but also in English translation. In addition to providing the usual components of the almanac, the *Grand Calendrier* was also a manual for life. It bore the text of the Creed, the Lord's Prayer and the Ten Commandments, and purported to include advice from a great sage, the shepherd of the high mountains. It tells the reader how to live a long, healthy and, above all, moral life, in constant meditation on death, striving always for sincerity and compassion. Like

An almanac seller plying his wares on the town square, advertising Jan van Vliet's *Almanac of Breda* (1664). Almanacs provided astrological predictions and a chronicle of historical events and wondrous apparitions.

most almanacs of its day, it emphasized the values of prudence and submission, and reinforced the existing social hierarchy.

In the eighteenth century, almanacs became more objective. Supporters of the Enlightenment despised their astrological prophecies. In the widely circulated Swiss almanac *Le Véritable messager boiteux* (The Veritable Lame Messenger), astrological content was outweighed by a record of important historical events. In the 1820s, Charles Knight of the Society for the Diffusion of Useful Knowledge produced his *British Almanac* with useful statistics and no astrology, but its tone was far too earnest and the book did not sell well. For the upper classes in Italy, there were fashion almanacs, court almanacs and almanacs for teaching good manners to the young. Elsewhere, there were medical almanacs and almanacs of proverbs. As long as they did not contain political news, almanacs escaped government surveillance. Today, one aspect of the genre survives in the daily newspaper horoscope.

Above: The *Grand Calendrier des bergers* (Shepherds' almanac) originated in the 1490s and was one of the most widely reproduced almanacs. Illustrated with many woodcuts, it provided a calendar together with homilies on vice and virtue, as well as advice on health and hygiene.

Left: Pages from an English almanac of 1677, published by George Larkin, showing religious festivals and the phases of the moon.

Walter Scott as a Global Bestseller

Until the late eighteenth century, the novel was regarded as an inferior genre of literature that did not offer moral instruction or ennobling sentiments. There were only a few exceptions to this rule: Alain-René Lesage's *Gil Blas*, Cervantes's *Don Quixote*, and the novels of Henry Fielding (1707–54) and Samuel Richardson (1689–1761), which commanded growing respect. But Walter Scott (1771–1832), more than any other single author, made the novel respectable. He became an internationally bestselling writer and a pillar of the nineteenth-century English literary canon alongside Charles Dickens (1812–70) and William Makepeace Thackeray (1811–63). Jane Austen (1775–1817) and George Eliot (1819–80) had meagre reputations in their day compared to Scott, Dickens and Thackeray, and during the Romantic period, Scott sold more novels than all other contemporary English novelists put together.

Sir Walter Scott invented the historical novel as we know it and his books became European bestsellers in his own lifetime. He also fuelled a romantic fashion for everything Scottish in the early nineteenth century.

In France and North America, Scott's success inspired many others to imitate the historical novel that he had pioneered. Honoré de Balzac's *Les Chouans* (1829) and the works of James Fenimore Cooper (1789–1851) were modelled on Scott's novels, and his taste for medievalism influenced Victor Hugo's *Notre-Dame de Paris* (The Hunchback of Notre-Dame) (1831). Scott was pirated, imitated and translated; his works were adapted for the stage and opera; and members of Parisian high society attended masked balls where guests dressed as characters from his *Waverley* novels.

During his early career, Scott and a school friend, James Ballantyne, established a print works and in 1809 formed a publishing house with James's brother John (Ballantyne & Co.), which produced much of Scott's popular poetry. This venture, together with the expense of maintaining his great baronial pile at Abbotsford in the Border country, drove Scott to the edge of bankruptcy. He was saved in 1813 by the publisher Archibald Constable & Co., who bought Ballantyne's unsold stock and in 1814 printed *Waverley*, Scott's first successful novel, anonymously.

In continental Europe, Scott was at first produced, like most novelists, in print runs of only 1,000 copies, but high demand pushed this up to 6,000 for the French version of *Woodstock* in 1826. The first French edition of Scott's complete works was produced in portable duodecimo format by Pierre-François Ladvocat and his partner Nicole between

Children re-enact a jousting tournament from Sir Walter Scott's *Ivanhoe*, one of Scott's most popular novels, in this painting by Charles Hunt from 1871.

1820 and 1828. From 1822 onwards, Gosselin was issuing French versions of new Scott novels simultaneously with their English originals. Altogether, twenty editions of Scott's complete works appeared in France from 1820 to 1851, with *Ivanhoe* and *Quentin Durward* (which was set in France) leading the way. He had similar success in Italy: in 1830, no fewer than five different series of Scott's novels were appearing from different publishers. In Germany, the novelist Willibald Alexis (1798–1871) produced a parody 'Scott' novel in 1823–24, entitled *Walladmor*, with Scott himself appearing as a character.

In North America, there was a similar scramble to get Scott's novels into print: Scott produced new titles so quickly and prolifically that publishers were forced to have them printed in sections by multiple printers simultaneously. Cornelius Van Winkle and Charles Wiley produced the first American edition of *Waverley* in 1815, in two volumes in duodecimo format. From 1819 onwards, Matthew Carey of Philadelphia was Scott's principal publisher in the USA.

English novelists from Defoe to Scott were very successful internationally in the late eighteenth and early nineteenth centuries. One factor in their popularity was their fresh subject matter: unlike their continental European competitors, which focused exclusively on the upper classes, English novels of this period included middle-class and even peasant characters. They also made a more direct emotional appeal to the audience: whereas educated European taste expected a literature of fine feeling without vulgarity or excess, English novels were intended to make their readers cry. Nevertheless, sometimes English novels had to be 'adapted' for continental European audiences, with offensive or extreme material removed. Auguste Defauconpret (1767–1843), Scott's prolific French translator, excised long sections from the originals: in *Les Puritains d'Écosse* (the French version of *Old Mortality*), for instance, he left out some arguments in favour of the Puritans.

A wood engraving of opera singer Jenny Lind (1820–87), nicknamed 'the Swedish nightingale', as Lucia di Lammermoor in Gaetano Donizetti's opera of the same name. The opera is based on Scott's novel *The Bride of Lammermoor*.

On the Margins of Europe

The publishing fever that afflicted western Europe had no parallel in southern and eastern Europe, where books were rare, and publishing was more traditional and dependent on the West. In Central Europe and the Baltic, German print culture was highly influential; in Greece, French and Italian books dominated. At the same time, the Ottoman and Russian empires were decisive cultural influences in the development of book production.

In the Ottoman empire, investment capital was in short supply and for some time the Orthodox Church did not fully embrace the benefits of printing. Until the eighteenth century, 80 per cent of Greek books were actually produced in Venice. These books were mainly liturgical works for Greek Orthodox worship, especially in the Venetian territories of Crete and the Ionian Islands. In the eighteenth century, the Orthodox clergy began to accept the value of printed books for educational purposes, and the rise of a Greek middle class created a market for secular books in Greek. The Venetian publishing industry was now in decline, and Vienna became the main centre for Greek book production.

After their expulsion from the Iberian peninsula in the 1490s, Jewish refugees had obtained permission from the Ottoman sultan Bayezid II to open print shops in Constantinople and Salonica, where they published Hebrew books. The Armenian minority enjoyed similar freedom under the Ottomans, and had four print shops in operation in Constantinople in the eighteenth century.

Catholic Croatia operated its own printeries from 1494, using the Cyrillic script named after the missionary Cyril who converted the Slavs to Christianity in the ninth century. With the consolidation of Ottoman power in the Balkans after the sixteenth century, Cyrillic printing shifted to Wallachia, which was permitted to become a centre for the printing of Slavonian and Romanian texts under episcopal control. Serbia, Bosnia and Herzegovina did

The *Octoechos* ('book of eight tones'), printed in the monastery of Cetinje in Montenegro in 1494, contained the order of Sunday service. It was one of the earliest liturgical works produced in Church Slavonic.

not have their own printing industries in the sixteenth century; they imported schoolbooks and religious texts from Russia or Hungary until the 1830s, when the development of early nineteenth-century nationalisms encouraged the production of literary works, dictionaries and grammars in national languages such as Czech, Slovakian, Hungarian and Ukrainian.

In eastern Europe, production of Slavic books remained completely under religious supervision until the reign of the reforming Tsar Peter the Great (1682–1725). In 1711 he set up a print shop in his new capital of St Petersburg, while the Russian Senate and the Academy of Sciences broke the clerical monopoly by producing scientific and scholarly works. Tsarina Catherine II tried to secularize book production further after 1783, and annual production reached a modest peak of 500 titles in 1788. But the French Revolution put an end to her tentative attempts at liberalization. Fear of unrest led to the closure of private print shops and the imposition of strict censorship rules throughout the Russian empire.

Above left: **The title page to an alphabet of 1705, showing the tsars of Russia.**

Above right: **This Sunday book was written by Sofronii Vrachanska, Bishop of Vratsa, and printed in Rimincy (Romania) in 1806. It was the first book printed in modern Bulgarian and offered spiritual guidance at a time when the Bible was not yet available in this language.**

4

THE PUBLISHER ARRIVES

Before 1830, the print run of an average novel rarely exceeded a few hundred copies. Stendhal's *Le Rouge et le Noir* (The Red and the Black), for instance, was published in 1830 with a run of only 750 copies. Stendhal dedicated his work to 'The Happy Few': it is hard to say if all his readers were happy, but they were certainly few, at least in his own lifetime. But by 1914 there was a mass market for cheap fiction, and readers all over France were familiar with his work. Social and economic changes had brought the typographical *ancien régime* to an end. Books and newspapers were mass produced, paper was as cheap as it would ever be, a working day of about ten hours gave people more leisure time and, in Western Europe at least, almost everyone could read.

In nineteenth-century Western Europe, the publisher came into his own as a specialist and an entrepreneur (in smaller European markets, these developments followed in the twentieth century). Until the early nineteenth century, the jobs of publishing, printing and bookselling had not been distinguished and many individuals combined all three functions. Now the publisher had arrived: he organized the finances, nurtured a stable of authors and devised marketing strategies. A few, such as Karl Baedeker and Pierre Larousse, became household names.

While the emergence of a mass reading public was a business opportunity for publishers, others saw it as a threat to society. How could the spread of socialist literature be stemmed? How could women be prevented from reading romantic fantasies that might undermine the stability of marriage?

The season of *étrennes* (New Year gifts) was a peak time for book sales in France. The publisher Hetzel regularly seized the moment to advertise his books for young readers, including novels by Jules Verne and his *Magasin d'éducation et de récréation*.

The Mechanization of Printing

Until the nineteenth century the simple wooden hand press continued to be used as it had since the invention of printing. Now the expansion of the market encouraged investment in more rapid processes that could supply larger print runs. Printing became increasingly mechanized, so that many more sheets could be produced at a faster rate. The printing world that Gutenberg had known had endured for almost four centuries; but after about 1830, it became unrecognizable. The wooden hand press co-existed with the first decades of industrialization, but from 1800, the new metal Stanhope presses became available. They had a longer working life than the old wooden presses, although they were considerably more expensive. The Stanhope press also had a large platen, which allowed the printer to ink a complete folio in a single operation. Friedrich Koenig (1774–1883) developed a steam-driven cylinder press in 1811 for the London *Times* that could print 1,100 sheets per hour. The traditional wooden press, if it were

The new Stanhope press pictured here was made of metal and had a large platen suitable for large-format productions such as newspapers. However, basic printing procedures remained largely unchanged.

working at full stretch, could only print at one tenth of this rate.

Mechanical presses started to proliferate after 1830. A rotary press appeared in Edinburgh in 1851 and was in use by the London *Times* in 1853. It was imported to France in 1866, to Germany in 1873 and to Spain in 1885. By the beginning of the twentieth century, rotary presses with multiple feeders could produce 48,000 pages per hour. From the 1870s, typesetting machines made production in large quantities both faster and cheaper. Paper-folding machines were created, and binding was mechanized by new cutting and binding equipment.

The manufacture of paper itself was revolutionized. Henry Fourdrinier (in 1799) and Thomas Gilpin (in 1816) produced paper-making machines that turned out paper in extremely wide continuous rolls. In the 1860s the extraction of paper from wood pulp rather than rags became technologically feasible, and the price of paper,

Above: The Applegarth press produced newsprint on a truly industrial scale. The London *Times* was an important investor in new printing technology.

Below: The huge Walter rotary press printed from curved stereotype plates and produced 10,500 copies per hour.

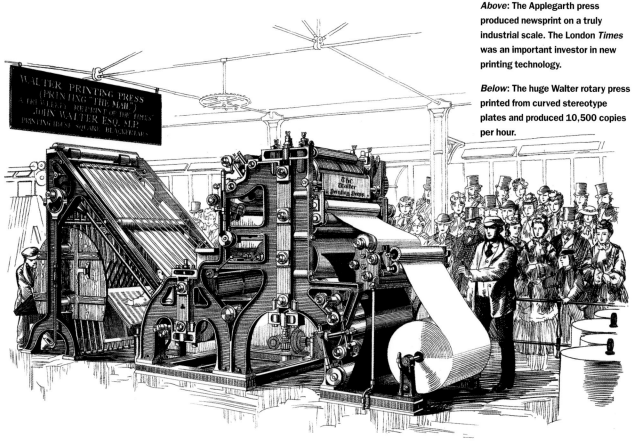

which had previously been a substantial outlay, fell progressively, drastically reducing the cost of book production. In France, the average price of a book fell by 50 per cent between 1840 and 1870. In Germany, which became a major supplier of industrial paper in the second half of the nineteenth century, raw materials made up about 30 per cent of production costs in 1870, but only 12 per cent in 1912.

Readers wanted their books to have pristine white pages, and during the latter half of the nineteenth century chlorine began to be added to the paper to achieve this. But bleached books were highly acidic, and therefore destined to self-destruct. Within a century the Bibliothèque Nationale de France realized that its 75,000 volumes from the period were decaying on the shelves. Some had to be destroyed, and others were microfilmed.

Mechanization did not transform the publishing world on its own; it was a necessary response to social and economic changes. Advances in basic literacy, culminating in the establishment of national systems of primary education at the end of the nineteenth century, ensured that the reading public was constantly expanding. Railway building, especially after the 1840s, made it more economical to supply books to a national market. After the introduction of Rowland Hill's Penny Post in England in 1840, postal services could bring periodicals and catalogues to all corners of the country. With these new opportunities for bookselling, mechanization helped to bring cheap literature to the masses.

A paper-making machine, pictured in 1853. In the second half of the nineteenth century, the manufacture of paper from wood pulp, and the mechanization of the process, brought down paper costs and made for much cheaper books.

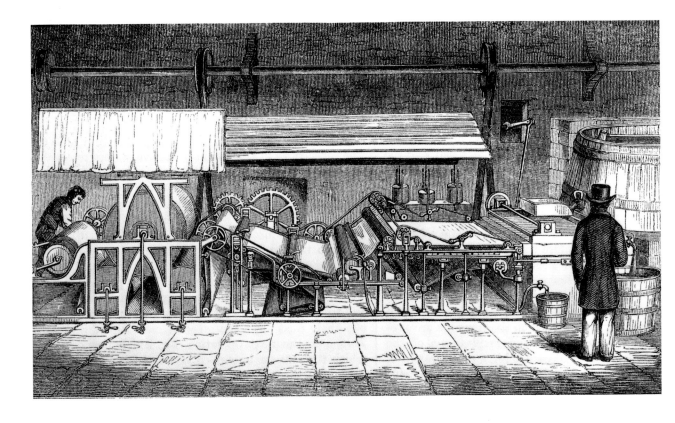

Nineteenth-century Book Illustrators

Until well into the nineteenth century, texts and images for the same book were produced by different processes in separate workshops. Three techniques for reproducing pictures co-existed: wood-engraving was the oldest; steel-engraving gave sharper definition and finer detail; lithography (invented by Alois Senefelder in 1819) allowed more textual variety and accuracy, as the artist could draw directly on to the printing plate itself. The newspaper industry favoured lithography; book illustrations used all three methods of reproduction, sometimes within a single volume.

The illustrator Gustave Doré (1832–83) began his career, at the age of fifteen, as a caricaturist for the French paper *Le Journal pour rire*. His preferred medium was wood-engraving, which he used to good effect in his illustrations for François Rabelais's classic grotesque novel *Gargantua et Pantagruel* in 1854. Doré's dark and sometimes grandiose visions adorned nineteenth-century fiction such as Honoré de Balzac's *Contes drolatiques* (Droll Stories) and Eugène Sue's *Le Juif errant* (The Wandering Jew). After the French public grew tired of his book illustrations, he was enthusiastically received in the USA and Britain, where his work was exhibited in a London gallery in 1868. When he died in 1883, he was working on illustrations for an edition of Shakespeare's plays.

Book illustration was becoming recognized as a fine art. The nineteenth-century fascination with natural history gave botanical and wildlife illustrators many exotic specimens to reproduce on

Gustave Doré produced 425 engravings for the 1855 edition of Balzac's *Contes drolatiques* (Droll Stories), a collection of burlesque tales first published in the 1830s.

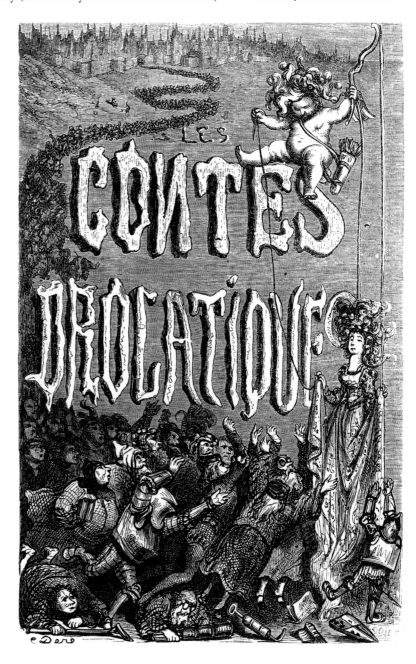

John James Audubon's *Birds of America* took flora and fauna illustration to a new level of sophistication. Images like this flamingo were reproduced life-size.

book plates. Two of the finest practitioners of this art were John James Audubon and John Gould.

Born in the French Caribbean, Audubon (1785–1851) spent his early life in France and Pennsylvania. After several business failures he toured the southern USA in the early 1820s, drawing bird life in pastel and watercolour. His work privileged texture, lively composition and dramatic poses over scientific accuracy, and consequently received a mixed response in America. But in Britain he gathered a number of influential subscribers and commissioned oil copies of his plates, which he sold to art collectors and naturalists. He published *Birds of America* (1827–38), an expensive collection of 435 hand-coloured aquatint pages. Known as 'the double elephant folio', the very large format of the book enabled him to produce life-size drawings of the birds. His next title, *Ornithological Biography* (1831–38), fully established his reputation as a specialist bird illustrator.

John Gould (1804–81) was a taxidermist who became curator and preserver for the London Zoological Society in 1828. Aware of the lucrative possibilities in illustrating the natural world, in the early 1830s he founded a publishing business with his wife, the artist Elizabeth Coxen (1804–41). She worked with a team of lithographers and colourists to transpose Gould's preparatory sketches on to finished plates. Gould produced *A Century of Birds from the Himalaya Mountains* (1831–32) and, after a two-year trip to Australia, the magnificent and costly *Birds of Australia* (1840), which was a milestone in Australian ornithology. He famously collaborated with Charles Darwin – it was Gould who first identified Darwin's Galápagos finches as a new species – authoring and illustrating the ornithological volume of Darwin's monumental *The Zoology of the Voyage of HMS Beagle* (1838–43).

John Gould had little formal education and was not a trained artist, but he saw the potential of lithography to produce high-quality colour plates, like this one of bower birds in his book *Birds of Australia*.

The Publisher's Role

Traditionally there had been no distinction between the printer, the publisher and the bookseller, but in the nineteenth century publishing roles became more specialized. In 1824, for instance, booksellers in Leipzig established their own professional association, the *Börsenverein des Deutschen Buchhandels*, the first to be independent from the printers' guilds. In the pre-industrial corporate structure of the industry, publishers and printers had often kept their jobs within the family, passing them on to sons or widows, thus creating dynasties of book-trade artisans. Now that the guilds no longer controlled entry to the profession, outsiders began to join their ranks. True, some publishers had previous experience as printers, but many others came from very different and perhaps very humble backgrounds. Successful publishers were self-made entrepreneurs with creative skills, independence and an appetite for risk-taking.

Calmann-Lévy's bookshop on the fashionable Boulevard des Italiens in Paris was a busy emporium, built on the Lévy brothers' profits from selling opera *libretti* and, later on, cut-price fiction.

The modern publisher had to have specialist knowledge of the market and make commercial decisions in the light of fluctuating demand. He had to organize capital backing for new ventures and series. He maintained connections with a stable of authors, determining the terms of their contracts and often seeing himself as a kind of intellectual patron. He took decisions about price, paper quality, format and advertising campaigns, and he had to coordinate networks of distribution. He did not need a specialized knowledge of typography to carry out these key functions; but he needed to be a leader with access to capital and the nerve to withstand the pressure of cut-throat competition.

Although the French industry was not the largest, it was in many ways the most dynamic. A stagnant population size imposed inherent limits on the growth of the French market, requiring greater ingenuity and invention from publishers if they were to expand their businesses. In the mid-century substantial businesses emerged, among them the house of Calmann-Lévy. The Lévy brothers, Michel (1821–75) and Calmann (1819–91), earned their early income from selling opera *libretti* and play scripts, successfully producing Henri Murger's *Vie de Bohème* in 1850 (on which Puccini based his opera). Their most important contribution to the history of publishing was a massive reduction in the price of books in 1856, when Michel Lévy inaugurated a new series of novels and poetry priced at only one franc per volume. The enormous profits of this pioneering venture enabled Lévy to open new offices near the Paris Opéra, and a bookshop on the very chic Boulevard des Italiens – an example of 'vertical concentration' in the industry, in which publishers tried to influence every level of production by buying up their own paper suppliers and retail outlets. The Lévy brothers put publishing at the forefront of the development of French capitalism, with investments in railways, insurance companies and public utilities in France, North Africa and the Austro-Hungarian empire.

These changes were paralleled in Britain, with the establishment of new publishing houses such as Macmillan, Murray and Longmans. With Macmillan as co-ordinator, British publishers imposed the Net Book Agreement of 1899, which governed the conditions under which they supplied books to bookshops, and tried to eliminate wildcat discounting.

Like the Lévys with their opera *libretti*, new publishers often became successful by exploiting a niche market. Karl Baedeker (1801–59), based in Koblenz from 1827, found his in travel guides, starting with his compact

German publisher Karl Baedeker found a lucrative niche market when he created his famous series of travel guides.

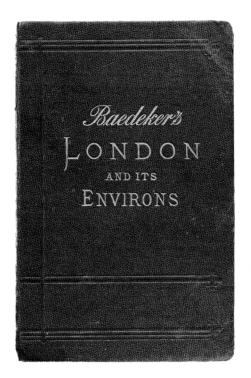

handbook to the Rhineland in 1835. Subsequent volumes on Belgium, the Netherlands, Switzerland, Germany and the Austro-Hungarian empire were all researched and written by Baedeker himself. These were the first in what would be a successful and enduring series of guidebooks, catering for well-heeled middle-class travellers. Baedeker's guides – known simply as 'Baedekers' – were distinguished by their red covers and star rating system for interesting attractions, hotels and restaurants. British publisher John Murray III (1808–92), who essentially invented the modern travel guide with his 'Murray Handbooks', was both Baedeker's role model and his chief competitor.

By the end of the nineteenth century, the publisher was a professional in his own right, and his expertise had become indispensable.

Left: The red binding and gold lettering were characteristic of the Baedeker brand. The guides were light and portable and the first to include detailed information about hotels and prices.

Below: Baedeker's guide to Austria, open at the map of Salzburg. Detailed maps replaced illustrations in these new practical guides.

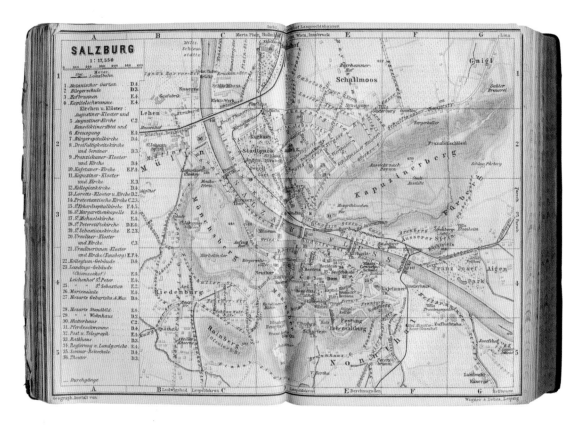

Copyright and Royalties

In the early nineteenth century, the royalty system as we now know it did not exist. In other words, authors' incomes were not in any way related to the actual sales of their work: publishers paid a lump sum for a manuscript and the author had no further claim to revenue. Sales of repeat editions, for which they paid the author nothing, were publishers' chief means of making a profit. Gradually the custom arose of paying authors according to the number of copies printed, but this was not the same as the number

ÉDITION DU FIGARO

PIERRE LOTI

Madame
Chrysanthème

Rossi

PARIS
CALMANN LÉVY, ÉDITEUR
3, RUE AUBER, 3

1888

A Calmann-Lévy edition of Pierre Loti's *Madame Chrysanthème*. The novel was one of a series in exotic settings by the bestselling French author. In its romanticization of the Far East it inspired Puccini's opera *Madame Butterfly*.

sold, and could prove expensive for a publisher if the book failed to sell. A true royalty system did not fully develop until the late nineteenth century, when international legislation was put in place to suppress pirate editions and recognize an author's copyright outside his or her home country.

A few authors would do almost anything to get published, which undermined the collective struggle to defend authors' rights. Émile Zola (1840–1902) made huge sacrifices in his early contracts. He secured a 10 per cent royalty from Lacroix, but agreed that the publisher could produce four times the usual number of royalty-free copies. He further agreed to receive his royalty in instalments, abandoned all rights to publication

Left: An 1859 poster for *Uncle Tom's Cabin* by Harriet Beecher Stowe, advertising several editions in English and German. Millions of copies were sold worldwide, but without international copyright the author earned relatively little.

Opposite: A poster from 1889 for a serialized illustrated edition of Émile Zola's novel *La Terre* (The Earth), a story about cunning, greedy peasants, first published in 1887. Instalments cost only 10 centimes each, but overall this was an expensive way to buy a novel.

in the press and at the same time committed himself to producing two novels a year for his publisher. By 1877, after the success of *L'Assommoir* (The Dram Shop), he was able to negotiate better terms, and Georges Charpentier granted him more than 14 per cent royalties and exclusive rights to serial publication in the press.

Harriet Beecher Stowe (1811–96) was paid only $400 for the initial newspaper serialization of *Uncle Tom's Cabin*, which would eventually become the bestselling novel of the nineteenth century, although the sum was still equivalent to more than three years' rent for the author. She received a 10 per cent royalty on the first book edition, published in 1852, and eventually earned $30,000 in royalties. While this was a substantial amount of money in the 1850s, it did not reflect the massive global sales of the book. Stowe earned nothing at all on editions sold in Britain and elsewhere, because there was no international copyright agreement in place at the time.

Such an agreement was already beginning to emerge, though it developed too slowly to benefit Stowe. During the 1850s individual countries signed bilateral treaties outlawing publishing piracy. In 1886 the Bern Convention for the Protection of Literary and Artistic Works – the first international copyright agreement – was signed in Bern, Switzerland, and the global economy of the book had come of age. For the first time, authors and publishers were protected against global publishing piracy. A mutually agreeable business model had been put in place that was to last over a century, until electronic publishing threw it into question.

By the end of the century, authors could expect to earn substantial sums from their literary works. French novelist Pierre Loti (1850–1923), for instance, was one of the best-paid writers of the period. The success of titles such as *Pêcheur d'Islande* (An Iceland Fisherman) (1886) and *Madame Chrysanthème* (1887) (a precursor to *Madame Butterfly*), set in the exotic locations he knew well as a naval officer, enabled him to secure royalties of between 17 and 21 per cent on the first popular editions of his works in the octodecimo format. Later editions, in larger and more expensive formats, attracted a lower royalty rate.

The Rise of the Bookstore

There were many ways of buying a book in the late nineteenth century. The traditional bookshop was only one of them; other shops sold books alongside groceries, hardware or haberdashery. In New England, the general store typically sold a few psalters and prayer books. There were street kiosks where Spanish readers could buy the latest fiction in instalments, and stalls, such as the *banchi* of Milan, that offered engravings, calendars, almanacs and religious brochures to passers-by. Itinerant hawkers carried a few books in their assorted baskets of wares. Nevertheless, dedicated bookstores were increasingly springing up in small towns and rural areas, spreading the reading habit and integrating the masses into mainstream metropolitan culture.

Bookselling was still a controlled profession. Both publishing and selling unauthorized literature risked fines and imprisonment under the system of censorship that Chancellor Klemens von Metternich tried to impose on Germany and the Austrian empire before 1848. In France, under the system created by Napoleon in 1810, a would-be bookseller had to apply for a licence (*brevet*), supplying four references certified by the local mayor testifying to his good morality, and four attestations of his professional capacity to perform the job. If the application was accepted, the new bookseller then had to swear

Opposite: Small children line up outside the Cologne teaching association bookshop while a customer examines the window display in this 1902 photograph. The Tonger music shop is just visible on the left.

Below: Interior view of Lackington's bookshop in Finsbury Square, north London, which was known as 'The Temple of the Muses'. It was said to be so spacious that a coach-and-four could drive around the circular counter. Lackington was an innovator: he printed enormous catalogues of his own stock and refused his customers credit.

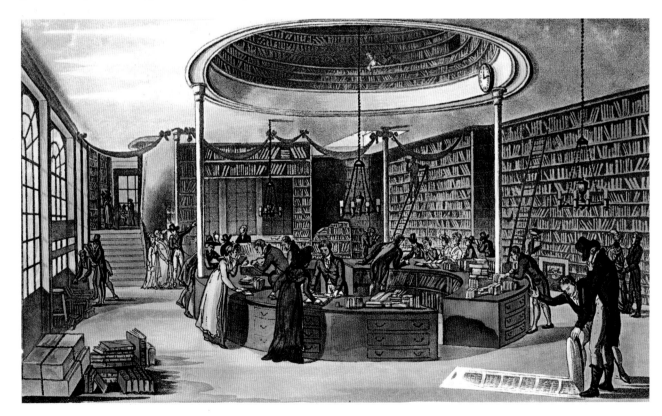

an oath of loyalty to the regime. The government wanted to be satisfied that the new bookshop would not be a centre for disseminating subversive publications, and that the business had enough capital to succeed. The *brevet* system was not relaxed until 1870.

Bookshop density was increasing steadily throughout the West. In Germany, for instance, there was a retail bookshop for every 10,000 inhabitants by 1895, rising to one for every 8,743 by 1910. The largest cities, as always, had more bookstores per capita than did rural and provincial areas: there was a bookshop for every 3,700 Berliners by 1913, and an astonishing one for every 1,700 Leipzig inhabitants by 1910. The rise in the number of bookshops was instrumental in consolidating national literary cultures. For the first time, every citizen was able to buy the same popular books, from well-known catechisms to novels such as *The Three Musketeers*.

Also in the nineteenth century, the railway bookstall brought books and newspapers to a new and even wider clientele. W. H. Smith (1825–91) established the first railway bookstall in London's Euston Station in 1848. Louis Hachette (1800–64) followed suit in 1852 with his Bibliothèques des Chemins de Fer, which the French government allowed to maintain a monopoly on rail-station bookselling. Hachette still owns the modern-day Relais chain of news-stands at French railway stations.

W. H. Smith's bookstall at King's Cross Station, London, in 1910. Smith was the first to see the potential of the railway bookstall. He had many imitators, including Louis Hachette in France.

Circulating and Lending Libraries

As new books remained expensive in the nineteenth century, private circulating libraries and public lending libraries allowed large numbers of readers access to reading material. The standard image of the circulating library was as the provider of sensational novels to women, but this was not always the case in practice. In many European countries, private circulating libraries catered for niche markets such as scientific groups and literary circles; in Britain they were more widespread, providing access to the latest fiction for a largely middle-class audience who could afford the substantial subscription fees. Readers from the lower classes relied on the free public libraries that began to be established by reformers, philanthropists and employers in the latter half of the nineteenth century with the aim of providing improving books for the masses.

The circulating libraries rented out bestsellers in large numbers, giving authors such as Walter Scott and Lord Byron even wider readerships than their impressive sales figures suggest. Far from regarding circulating libraries as a threat to their business, publishers saw them as reliable customers who ordered large quantities of books in bulk for their many customers. In return, the publishers offered the circulating libraries substantial discounts. Mudie's Select Library, for instance, which was established in Britain in 1842, enjoyed up to a 50 per cent discount on purchases; it was also instrumental in encouraging the 'three-decker novel' – published in three volumes so that three customers could hire different parts of it at the same time. Circulating libraries therefore kept book prices high: so long as Mudie's took between 800 and 1,000 copies of a new title, even at a high discount, the publisher had little incentive to produce books in the less-expensive single-volume format.

A portrait of Susanna Oakes, keeper of the circulating library in Ashbourne, Derbyshire, drawn *c.* 1800. Circulating libraries catered primarily for readers of popular fiction and provided employment for single women, widows and retirees.

Corbuns Library

Dorchester

S U S A N N A   O A K E S

KEEPER OF THE CIRCULATING LIBRARY AT ASHBORNE
IN THE COUNTY OF DERBY.

Kitty take those books to the library and get M.ʳˢ Brown to change them; tell her I'm fond of the *rumantic*.

The circulating library trade was not without its perils: bestselling fiction titles went out of fashion quickly and a company could be left sitting on a large pile of unusable stock. During the late 1880s and early 1890s, the rising popularity of cheap reprints, costing a fraction of an annual library subscription, put organizations such as Mudie's out of business for good.

Public libraries, meanwhile, were experiencing a renaissance. Until they were taken over by nineteenth-century reformers, public libraries had existed primarily to conserve ancient treasures, admitting only scholars and erudite amateurs, and restricting access to just a few hours per week. In the nineteenth century, however, the rise of literacy and (in some countries) the extension of voting rights made the ruling classes realize that what ordinary people read was a matter of public interest. Providing healthy literature through more openly accessible libraries became a priority for reformers and politicians alike. When Charles Dickens officially opened the Manchester Free Public Library in 1852, he made a grand speech expressing the hope that books might neutralize conflicts between capital and labour. A few years later, the Cotton Famine struck the manufacturing centres of Lancashire and put many men out of work, but no great agitation or revolt ensued. Many international observers concluded that Britain had found the secret to successful social control, and the accessible public library was one way to achieve it.

Britain had a head start in lending library provision. Since 1850, local authorities had been permitted to levy local taxation to finance libraries, and the rate was doubled in 1855. The result could be seen, for example, in the northern city of Leeds, which in 1902 had a central public library with fourteen local branches serving a population of less than half a million people. Elsewhere, private enterprise played a similar role in

Left: A reader from the 1830s, obviously keen on her romantic novels and warm alcoholic beverages, calls out: 'Kitty take those books to the library and... change them...I'm fond of the rumantic'.

Below: Numbered admission tokens from Plymouth Free Library, Devon. Plymouth residents voted to establish the library in 1871 and it was set up by private subscriptions supported by local government funds.

increasing popular access to books. In Germany enormous book-lending businesses emerged by the end of the century, including Borstell & Reimarus, which in 1891 was offering 600,000 volumes for rent in its four-storey premises in Berlin, where its customers included Prince Bismarck.

Private philanthropy funded new library buildings in the USA. Andrew Carnegie (1835–1919), a poor Scottish migrant who became a millionaire steel manufacturer, helped to finance about 1,600 new public libraries between 1886 and 1917. Carnegie never provided total funding for any project; he believed local authorities should make their own effort and demonstrate the self-determination to which he attributed his own spectacular success. Many Carnegie libraries were built in the neoclassical style with imposing pillars and a tidy lawn, conveying reverence for the printed word. Despite the elegance of the buildings, local residents did not always relish the prospect of a public library in their neighbourhood, as it brought working-class and black customers into sedate middle-class districts.

By the end of the nineteenth century, employers began to see value in providing libraries in the workplace. Employees could find the resources to study for exams leading to promotion, and it was thought that reading might improve their morality and sense of cooperation. Department stores created libraries for their employees, and factory

The Carnegie Library in Pittsburgh, Pennsylvania, with an inscription proclaiming its democratic mission. The imposing classical front was designed to convey dignity, but not every reader saw it as welcoming.

Develop the Power
that is within you

Get ahead. Books are free
at your Public Library

A poster from 1921 promoting working-class reading. In spite of the best intentions of lending libraries, only a minority of workers wished to read self-improving books.

libraries sprang up, soon to be rivalled by trade union libraries. Krupp's library in Essen, Germany, established in 1899, had over 61,000 volumes by 1909, and 50 per cent of workers used them. Port Sunlight, Bourneville and Rowntree had similar schemes in Britain, as did Ford and Goodyear in the USA. In Australia, the New South Wales Railway and Tramway Institute issued over 900,000 loans annually at its peak in 1929, which made it the largest lending library in the country.

The trouble, as far as the library reformers were concerned, was that library users overwhelmingly demanded popular fiction rather than edifying literature and educational books. Ninety per cent of the loans issued by the New South Wales Railway Institute during the 1920s were of fiction. Earnest librarians were disappointed: the masses wanted entertainment, not instruction.

The World of the Brothers Grimm

Brothers Jakob (1785–1863) and Wilhelm (1786–1859) Grimm were academics at the University of Göttingen. They were members of the German Romantic generation in an era when Germany itself was not yet a unified nation state, but its national identity was already emerging in German language and literature. The German philosopher Johann Gottfried von Herder (1744–1803) formulated the idea that a nation's distinctive soul could be found in its peasant culture ('the *Volk*'). Inspired by Herder, the Grimms set out to transform the oral folktales of German peasants into a great national literature that would express the essence of German-ness.

At least, that was the idea. In practice, the Grimms' famous collections of folk stories, first published in 1812 as *Kinder- und Hausmärchen* (Children's and Household Tales), did not accurately represent the peasant bedrock of German culture. Instead of

Jakob and Wilhelm Grimm listen to the storyteller Dorothea Viehmann in Niederzwehren, Germany. Dorothea was the daughter of an innkeeper and a living source for the Grimms' folktales. She was descended from Huguenot refugees and many of her tales actually had French origins.

transcribing stories directly from German peasants, the Grimms consulted their own immediate literary circle in Hesse. Some of their informants were not even of German ancestry, and many were influenced by the fairy tales of Charles Perrault (1628–1703), first published in seventeenth-century France. Although the Grimms' collection was received enthusiastically in a spirit of German nationalism, it owed much to French precedents.

In adapting their source tales, the Grimms invented many princes and princesses, and toned down suggestions of domestic conflict. In the fourth edition of *Hansel and Gretel*, for example, published in 1840, the children's mother became a stepmother so as to make the parents' abandonment of their offspring more explicable. Although the Grimms sanitized much, they were not averse to adding violent details to ensure that villains received the punishment they deserved. At the end of Perrault's version of *Cinderella*, for instance, the two ugly stepsisters are forgiven by the heroine and accompany her to the prince's court, where they are married to lords, but in the Grimms' retelling their eyes are pecked out by pigeons as they depart for Cinderella's wedding.

The cover of a Berlin edition of Grimm's fairy tales, published in 1865. The fairy and her menagerie give no hint of the violence present in many of the stories.

The brothers' first collection comprised eighty-six stories, to which were added another seventy in the subsequent volume published in 1814. Altogether seven editions were published during their lifetimes, and the collection gradually expanded to include 211 tales in all. Although they started life as monuments to a distinctively German literature, the Grimms' stories have a universal appeal and were regularly republished in many different languages throughout the nineteenth and twentieth centuries.

Novels by the Month

The serialization of fiction gave authors and publishers new avenues for reaching readers. There were two distinct forms of serialization: firstly, publishing in single stand-alone instalments, which was popular in the mid-nineteenth century; secondly, the *roman-feuilleton* and its successors, which appeared in newspapers in the early nineteenth century and in monthly magazines in the later decades of the century. Although fiction dominated the serials, almost anything could be serialized, and usually was: encyclopaedias, memoirs of celebrities such as François-René de Chateaubriand, and even Karl Marx's *Das Kapital*.

The *roman-feuilleton* made fortunes for those who knew how to maximize the suspense and anticipation that an episodic structure allowed. In France, Eugène Sue (1804–57) and Alexandre Dumas (1802–70) were masters of the genre. Dumas's *The Three Musketeers* (1844) appeared first as a *feuilleton*, as did *The Count of Monte Cristo* (1844–46), which its author managed to stretch out to 139 separate instalments. From mid-1844 to mid-1855, Sue's serial *Le Juif errant* (The Wandering Jew) increased the circulation of *Le Constitutionnel* from 3,600 to 25,000. Production in book form followed immediately: the novel – considered interminable and nearly unreadable by modern standards – went through twenty-seven editions by 1880.

Serialization was the main reason that nineteenth-century novels were so long: authors were paid by the line and by the episode. If a title was successful, it was in the author's and publisher's interests to keep the story going for as long as possible,

The Three Musketeers, first published in 1844, became one of the best-known novels of the late nineteenth century. This front cover adorned an edition that was published in instalments.

but if a serial was unpopular, it might be prematurely axed, or the author told to wind it up quickly. Frederick Marryat's English children's book, *The Children of the New Forest*, for instance, later one of his most popular novels, first appeared in serial form in 1847 but it was cancelled after the first monthly issue.

An edition by instalments of *Le Comte de Monte Cristo* (The Count of Monte Cristo) by Alexandre Dumas, first published between 1844 and 1846. The cover shows the heroine Mercédès, the cell of the Abbé Faria on the left, and the escape of the hero Edmond Dantès from the Château d'If on the right.

Not every writer could keep up with the hectic pace of serial writing, which demanded as many as 20,000 words per month. Wilkie Collins (1824–89), for instance, was never much more than a week ahead of publication. Dumas, on the other hand, was a writing factory: he would work twelve to fourteen hours a day with his collaborator Auguste Maquet, writing several novels simultaneously for serialized publication.

Publishers now routinely began to produce new novels in several different formats: a serialized version – either printed in a journal or sold as stand-alone booklets through bookshops – followed by a three-decker library version and then, after a short interval, a cheaper reprint on inferior paper. Perhaps an even cheaper reprint would follow, costing sixpence or a few centimes. Many of the great works of the nineteenth century followed this publishing trajectory. In the USA, *Uncle Tom's Cabin* first appeared in 1851–52 as a serial in the *National Era*, a weekly anti-slavery journal. In Russia, illustrated weeklies such as *Niva* serialized the works of Ivan Turgenev (1818–83), Maxim Gorky (1868–1936) and Anton Chekhov (1860–1904) in twenty-four-page tabloid format.

In Britain, Charles Dickens (1812–70) issued nine of his novels issued in monthly instalments, starting with *The Pickwick Papers*, published by Chapman & Hall in 1836–37. In 1852–53, *Bleak House* sold 40,000 copies in monthly instalments costing one shilling each. In 1850, Dickens launched his own two-penny magazine, *Household Words*, succeeded in 1859 by his new journal *All the Year Round*, which had a weekly circulation of 100,000, boosted by the success of *A Tale of Two Cities* (1859). *All the Year Round* also published Dickens's *Great Expectations* (1860–61) and Wilkie Collins's *The Woman in White* (1859–60). Dickens was exceptional in making serialization pay over several decades. Although his contemporary William Makepeace Thackeray (1811–63) was successful with the serialized version of *Vanity Fair*, produced by Bradbury & Evans in 1847–48, *The Virginians* (1857–59) proved a relative flop in the same format, after which Thackeray gave up this form of publication.

Buying a novel in instalments was extremely expensive compared to a single-volume work, but the advantage for both reader and publisher was that the cost was spread out over a year or two. After the 1860s, however, there was no longer room in the market for novels sold as stand-alone instalments, because so many magazines regularly carried serialized fiction and the cheapest reprints were now within the reach of modest budgets.

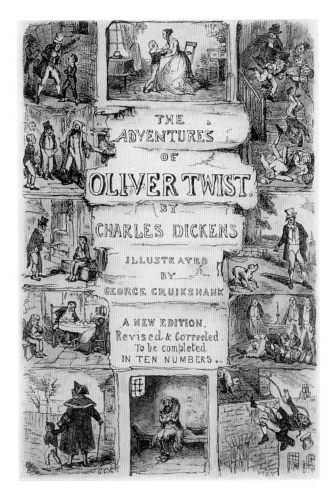

The cover of Charles Dickens's *Oliver Twist*, illustrated by George Cruikshank. The novel first appeared in ten monthly instalments in *Bentley's Miscellany* between 1837 and 1839. Unlike other novelists, Dickens persisted with instalment publishing for nine of his books.

Dime Novels

In 1860, the New York publishers Erastus (1821–94) and Irwin (1826–82) Beadle launched a new series of cheap and compact paperbacks, measuring approximately 10 × 15 cm (4 × 6 in.), entitled Beadle's Dime Novels. The name became the general term for a wide range of sensational pulp fiction produced by different publishers in pocket-size editions up to the early twentieth century.

The Beadle brothers' first title was a reprint of a sentimental novel by a well-known author, Ann S. Stephens (1810–86). In her *Malaeska, the Indian Wife of the White Hunter* (1860), a young Native American woman faced insurmountable odds after the death of her white soldier husband. The story of her sad fate sold more than 65,000

American dime novels and pulp-fiction magazines of the late nineteenth century, including the popular Nick Carter detective stories and the Beadle brothers' title *The Blue Anchor* in its distinctive pale orange cover.

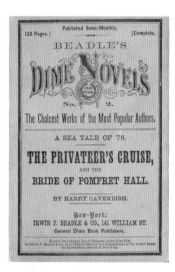

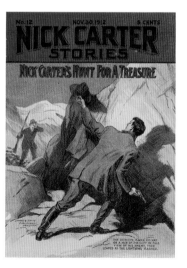

copies within the first few months of its publication as a dime novel. Further Beadle Dime Novels appeared monthly, and then fortnightly. They were printed on poor-quality paper and their length rarely exceeded 35,000 words. First produced in orange-pink wrappers, they were given hand-stencilled colour covers from 1874. Their sensational stories, low price (ten cents, by definition) and lurid covers made them hugely attractive to young working-class readers, although these were not their only fans.

Many dime novels were original works; others were reprinted from newspapers or magazines. Dime novelists included journalists, teachers and lawyers who wrote to conventional storylines on a weekly basis, often under multiple pseudonyms. Better-known writers such as Robert Louis Stevenson (1850–94), Bret Harte (1836–1902) and Louisa May Alcott (1832–88) were also enlisted. Adventures at sea and romances were prominent among the earliest titles, but the most popular stories involved conflicts between white settlers and Native Americans in the Wild West. The Beadles' second major success was *Seth Jones, or the Captives of the Frontier*, in which an intrepid white hunter, dressed in the obligatory buckskins and coonskin cap, rescues several white prisoners from the Mohawks. The book, by nineteen-year-old schoolmaster Edward S. Ellis (1840–1916), reportedly sold 600,000 copies. Buffalo Bill was another Western hero of many dime novels authored first by Edward Judson (under the pen-name 'Ned Buntline') (1813–86) and later by Colonel Prentiss Ingraham (1843–1904).

By the 1880s the content of the dime novel was beginning to reflect the increasing urbanization of American society. The frontier adventurer was giving way to detectives and espionage agents, and heroines working in city settings. The popularity of amateur detective Nick Carter led Street & Smith to issue three different series of his adventures between 1891 and 1915. His creator, Frederic Van Rensselaer Dey (1861–1922), could not keep up with demand and additional authors were hired to ensure a constant output.

The popularity of the dime novel began to decline in the 1890s, as conventional novels became more affordable and even less expensive pulp-fiction magazines arrived on the scene. After the First World War, customers had many other forms of light entertainment to choose from, including movies and radio.

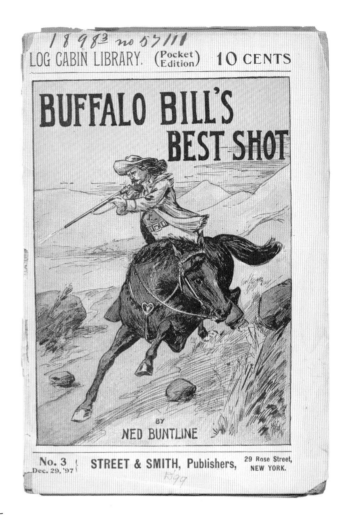

Buffalo Bill and his legendary marksmanship were the subject of many dime novels such as this one authored by the pseudonymous 'Ned Buntline'. The story first appeared in the *New York Weekly* in 1872. However, the frontier world where Buffalo Bill thrived was already disappearing fast.

The Russian *lubki*

The *lubok* (plural *lubki*) was the Russian equivalent of the chapbook. In contrast to chapbooks in Western Europe, *lubki* remained popular well into the early twentieth century, due to the slow development of literacy and high rate of poverty in Tsarist Russia. Religious works made up half of the repertoire until the 1890s, when secular *lubki* began to dominate. The corpus included portraits of the tsar, tales of great battles, accounts of drunken carnivalesque orgies, bandit adventures and popular folktales such as the stories of the witch Baba Yaga.

The sheer volume of *lubok* production was staggering. After 1895, production tripled to reach 32,000 titles in 1914, in all languages spoken in the Russian empire, with a total circulation of 130 million. The format of the *lubok* was similar to that of the broadsheet, combining a text with a woodcut image, which was later replaced by a lithograph hand-coloured by skilled workers. Colouring *lubki* prints was a thriving cottage industry in the Moscow region during the eighteenth century, until chromolithography eventually made the process redundant.

Lubki production was concentrated in Moscow around Nikolskaya Street; their main point of sale was the Spassky Bridge, alongside religious wares. *Lubki* authors were often peasants; some of the publishers, too, were ex-peasants. I. D. Sytin (1851–1934), the son of a peasant, became the largest publisher in Russia, with a virtual monopoly of the *lubki* market by 1914. He dealt with thousands of booksellers, using the annual fair at Nizhni Novgorod as a distribution hub.

This Russian woodcut illustrates a folk story about the witch Baba Yaga and a bald man. Millions of such *lubki* prints were sold in the Tsarist period.

The pre-revolutionary intelligentsia saw *lubki* as politically backward works that distorted true peasant values, as they promoted loyalty to the tsar and frequently expressed anti-Semitic and pro-Orthodox views. Some intellectuals blamed the failings of the *lubok* on the evils of capitalism; socialists, in particular, looked forward to publishing more enlightened forms of popular literature that would not be enslaved to market forces. After the 1917 Revolution, there was no place for *lubki*.

A Russian illustrated sheet proclaiming that 'Hops are head above all other fruit'.

Japanese Prints of the Floating World

Ukiyo-e were Japanese woodblock prints produced in the city of Edo (Tokyo) between the seventeenth and twentieth centuries, using a style and technique popularized by the printmaker Hishikawa Moronobu in the 1670s. The prints formed an established tradition depicting the 'floating world' of kabuki theatre, teahouses, geishas and courtesans – all the sophisticated entertainments of urban society. Later *ukiyo-e* included striking portrayals of natural landscape. At first the images were drawn in ink and hand-coloured afterwards. In the eighteenth century, polychrome printing was used to make full-colour reproductions called *nishiki-e.*

Often prints originated as theatre posters or advertisements for brothels, but in many cases they were gathered together for publication in book form, each print carrying the

One of the many woodblock prints Hokusai produced in the 1830s for his two famous series, 'Thirty-six Views of Mount Fuji' and 'One Hundred Views of Mount Fuji'.

A Tokyo street scene with Mount Fuji in the background, from Utagawa Hiroshige's 'One Hundred Famous Views of Edo', 1856. In contrast to Hokusai, Hiroshige (1797–1858) specialized in scenes depicting daily life and human activities.

signature of the artist. They became a mass medium, bought by those who wanted a pin-up of a favourite teahouse hostess or sumo wrestler.

Katsushika Hokusai (1760–1849) was among the most celebrated artists and printmakers of the later Edo period. His series, with the self-explanatory title 'Thirty-six Views of Mount Fuji', was published in 1831; it included the print *The Great Wave off Kanagawa*, which became a very popular image in the West. Mount Fuji had special meaning for Hokusai, who belonged to a Buddhist sect that revered the mountain as a source of eternal life.

In the Meiji period (after the 1860s), Japan became more open to Western cultural influences and photography began to make *ukiyo-e* obsolete. European artists prized them, however; the influence of Japanese prints on the art of Claude Monet (1840–1926), for example, is inescapable.

Plum branches beside bookshelves and a writing desk, in a rice-paper woodblock print by Gogaku Yajima, dating from between 1815 and 1820.

Masters of Mass Fiction

At the end of the nineteenth century, a mass market in fiction had developed. Publishers became adept at producing works in various formats and at different prices, reprinting at judicious intervals, in order to maximize the potential of different markets. Popular novelists produced copy at breakneck speed and recycled tried and tested formulas. Serious literary critics deplored their bad taste, but their works sold in enormous quantities. Among the most prominent of these masters of mass fiction were Karl May in Germany, Jules Verne in France and Marie Corelli in Britain.

Karl May (1842–1912) wrote Westerns featuring a German character, Old Shatterhand, and the Apache warrior Winnetou. Old Shatterhand appeared in sixteen of his novels, which May usually narrated in the first person. May was born in Saxony and never in fact visited the western USA, but his novels included all the traditional elements of Westerns, portraying a pre-industrial world where individuals were independent and traditional masculine values were respected.

May's global sales have been estimated at 200 million copies. His novels appealed to young working-class male readers and were condemned by the intellectual elite. In 1899, his works were banned from Bavarian secondary schools on the grounds that they were too trashy and sensational to be appropriate reading matter for students. May's modern reputation has been tarnished unfairly by the association of his works with the chauvinistic nationalism of early twentieth-century Germany. May himself became increasingly Christian and pacifist, but the re-editions of his novels produced after his death by Karl May Verlag during the Third Reich included racist overtones not present in the originals. In fact, 88 per cent of all Karl May sales were achieved *after* 1945.

The Apache warrior Winnetou, seen here in an illustration of 1904, was the creation of German author Karl May. Now largely forgotten, May was a master of pulp fiction who enjoyed high popularity over many decades.

· KARL · MAY ·

·· WINNETOU ·

Jules Verne (1828–1905) also appealed strongly to adolescent males, although his publisher Jules Hetzel marketed Verne not as an adventure novelist, but as a writer of educational fiction who popularized scientific discoveries and recent historical events such as the American Civil War, which provided the backdrop of *Nord et Sud* (1887). His novels reflect the endemic misogyny and racism of his time: he was accused of anti-Semitism for his unflattering portrayal of a German Jewish trader in *Hector Servadac* (1877), and in *Le Tour du monde en quatre-vingts jours* (Around the World in 80 Days) (1873), he described the slaughter of Native Americans without compunction.

Hetzel was careful to make Verne palatable to his French and foreign audiences. He added religious references: Captain Nemo's dying words in *Vingt mille lieues sous les mers* (Twenty Thousand Leagues Under the Sea) (1869) became 'Dieu et Patrie!' – God and the Motherland! He deleted entire chapters, sometimes inserting his own versions, rearranged Verne's text and often persuaded him to change his plots entirely. Meanwhile, he developed a profitable publishing strategy for Verne's novels. First came the bimonthly episodes in his *Magasin d'éducation et de récréation*. Then he issued an edition of the complete novel in a portable format, without illustrations, with an initial run of 30,000 copies. This would often be followed by an illustrated presentation edition, suitable as a New Year's gift, with the luxurious gold and red bindings that still make Verne's collected *Voyages Extraordinaires* one of the most attractive achievements of French publishing. Frequently there was a fourth version of the book produced for a new audience: a play adapted from the novel, if not an opera with music by Jacques Offenbach, as in the case of his *Le Voyage dans la Lune*, based on Verne's *De la Terre à la Lune* (From the Earth to the Moon) (1865).

Marie Corelli (1855–1924) was despised by literary critics, but at the peak of her popularity in the 1890s her novels

Hetzel's publishing strategy for Jules Verne was first to serialize the work in his own children's magazine and then follow up with a large-format, single-volume book, bound in striking red and gold covers. One of these was *Famille Sans Nom* (A Family Without a Name) from 1889, Verne's tale of a family during the Lower Canada Rebellion of 1837.

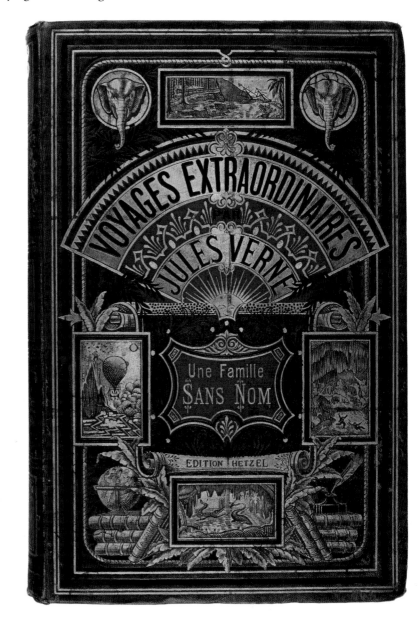

MISS MARIE CORELLI IN HER GONDOLA "THE DREAM" ON THE AVON

sold 100,000 copies a year – a figure of which her contemporaries Arthur Conan Doyle and H. G. Wells could only dream. Her plots combined a burning religiosity and firm sense of morality with passionate and mildly erotic love scenes. Melodramatic or not, *The Sorrows of Satan*, published by Methuen in 1895, was in its sixtieth edition by 1924. *The Master Christian* (1900) told the story of the second coming of Christ in the person of a street urchin named Manuel, who remains unacknowledged by the Roman Catholic Church. Eminent clergymen gave sermons on Corelli's work.

London-born Corelli's real name was Mary ('Minnie') Mackay, but she claimed Venetian descent, scattered French and Italian phrases quite freely in her novels – sometimes even correctly – and hired a gondola, complete with gondolier, for cruises on the Avon at Stratford. Today it is hard to fathom the appeal of her emotional extravagance – George Bentley, who published her first six titles, tried to curb her verbosity and told her not to write too fast – but Queen Victoria ordered all her books, and the mystically inclined Empress Alexandra of Russia is also reported to have been among her fans. Corelli's reputation began to decline during the First World War, when she was fined for unpatriotically hoarding sugar, and she alienated part of her audience by publishing a book and series of pamphlets expressing her disapproval of the women's suffrage movement.

British novelist Marie Corelli knew that self-advertisement would do no harm to sales of her romantic and emotionally charged bestsellers. In this scene she is seen relaxing in her personal gondola on the River Avon.

5 KNOWLEDGE FOR ALL

The first half of the twentieth century was a dark period in world history, and a troubled time in the history of the book. Wars, economic depression, paper shortages and higher labour costs ensured that the boom of the late nineteenth century would not be repeated. This was the century of genocides, in which millions died and brutal attempts were sometimes made to obliterate their history and culture, as embodied in books and libraries. Yet throughout these hard times, readers developed an insatiable demand for escapist pulp fiction. After the Second World War, book production recovered, book clubs rose in popularity, and the modern publishing industry took shape in the West and the East. The digital revolution was just around the corner.

The impact of computerization is often compared to that of Gutenberg's invention of printing – mistakenly so, because printing never changed the physical form of the codex, whereas computerization has already enacted a complete transformation of the way we transmit, consume and interact with texts. The internet has put an unprecedented amount of knowledge at our fingertips, creating exciting new possibilities as well as presenting authors and publishers with new challenges. Hand-held reading devices compete with the traditional codex, and the utopian fantasy of a single book containing all the knowledge of the world within its covers may one day literally be within our grasp.

Female Muslim students at a bookstall at Nilkhet book market in Dhaka, Bangladesh.

New Technologies

By the mid-nineteenth century, printing had been mechanized, and paper was being produced for the first time on an industrial basis. Only one bottleneck remained: the labour-intensive task of composition. For centuries, compositors had assembled the type by hand, character by character. Towards the end of the nineteenth century, new techniques were introduced in the USA that hugely accelerated the process.

In 1884 Ottmar Mergenthaler (1854–99) invented his Linotype machine, a 'hot metal' typesetting system that cast entire lines of type from molten lead injected into moveable matrices. The operator used a ninety-character keyboard to assemble the matrices in the correct order, eliminating the need to assemble, remove and sort individual pre-cast characters by hand. A single worker using a Linotype machine could set 8,000 characters per hour, whereas the very best compositor using traditional methods could not improve on 1,500. Linotype suited newspaper production very well, but it was not ideal for books, which typically had wider type columns than newspapers, as well as higher editorial standards: proof correction was difficult when lines were cast as single pieces of type. Tolbert Lanston's Monotype machine, which was introduced in 1887–89, overcame this obstacle, adapting the Linotype process to cast entire lines of moveable type in a single operation.

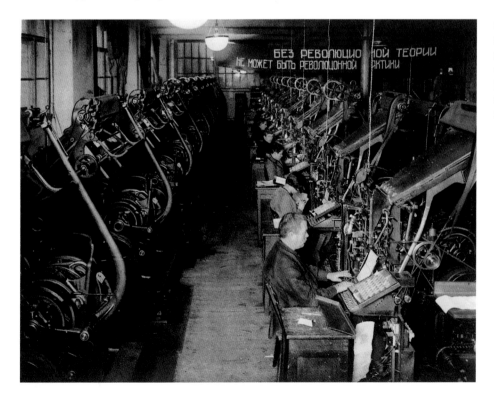

Linotypists at work at the Soviet newspaper *Pravda*. The mechanization of typesetting cleared a bottleneck on the production line and was highly suitable for large-circulation newspapers.

With the introduction of this technology, global book production surged. By 1909 Britain, with its lucrative overseas markets, was producing over 10,000 titles per year. France produced more than 13,000 book titles annually by the end of the nineteenth century, even as war and political unrest caused serious interruptions to economic life. Italian book production before the First World War ran at an annual average of 9,250 titles. But by far the largest producer of books was Germany. From the late nineteenth century until the start of the First World War, German publishers enjoyed a period of unprecedented growth, reaping full benefit from mechanization, falling production costs and the creation of a single national market. In 1884 annual German book production was running at over 15,000 titles, and by 1913 Germany had become the biggest world producer of books. In France, however, production reached a peak and the market appeared saturated by 1900, which resulted in a spate of discount selling to unload surplus stock in the years before the First World War. Britain weathered the pre-war downturn rather better, as its important export markets, such as Australia, compensated for the levelling-off in home demand.

With this global surge in production, the book was transformed into a mass-produced consumer product during the late nineteenth and early twentieth centuries. Covers became more lurid as sophisticated colour illustration became technologically feasible and inexpensive. The choice of typefaces was increasingly limited, however, as the new automated printing machines used only a small number of standardized fonts. Meanwhile, new outlets developed to bring these mass-produced books to wider markets, and the traditional bookshop began to lose its pre-eminent position to department stores and book clubs.

Above: The Lanston Monotype was patented in Philadelphia in 1887. It improved on the Linotype machine by allowing manual correction of individual characters, which made for greater accuracy.

Left: By the time this revised and enlarged 1890 edition of *Mrs Beeton's Every-Day Cookery and Housekeeping Book* was published, colour printing could be achieved on the spine. The first edition of this immensely successful work appeared in 1861, when Isabella Beeton was only twenty-five.

The Romance of the Encyclopaedia

In the nineteenth century, a few ambitious individuals had the idea of encapsulating all the world's knowledge within a single book. They envisaged encyclopaedias that would be universal and accessible, and would serve as tools for educating the general public. The desire to popularize knowledge via reference books already had a rich eighteenth-century ancestry: France had produced the great encyclopaedias of Denis Diderot and Charles-Joseph Panckoucke; in Britain, Ephraim Chambers published his first *Cyclopaedia* in London in 1728. Nineteenth-century encyclopaedias celebrated modernity and put greater emphasis on political and cultural identity than did their predecessors.

Above: James Murray working on the *Oxford English Dictionary* in the shed he called his 'scriptorium', surrounded by thousands of slips of paper containing items which were being considered for inclusion.

The *Encyclopaedia Britannica*, first published in Edinburgh, combined short entries and definitions with specialized essays on the arts and social sciences. The first edition appeared in weekly instalments between 1768 and 1771; the second, in ten volumes between 1777 and 1784. In the earliest editions, most of the entries were written by

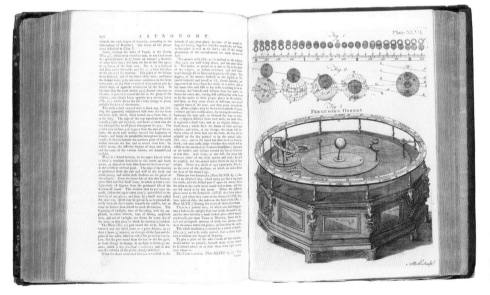

Left: Pages from the *Encyclopaedia Britannica*, which was published from 1768 onwards and became a national institution.

William Smellie (1740–95), the editor of the project, but the encyclopaedia was soon profitable enough to hire prominent scholars to write entries on their individual specialities. A century later, at the height of the British empire, the *Britannica* was the 'national encyclopaedia', commanding the services of many expert contributors.

In France, Pierre Larousse (1817–75) sacrificed his health in producing the *Grand dictionnaire universel du XIXe siècle*. Larousse was a blacksmith's son who became a schoolteacher but retired early to follow his dream. His dictionaries were secular in spirit and were put on the Catholic Index of Prohibited Books. Meanwhile, the anti-clerical Larousse lived unmarried with his companion Suzanne Caubel and vowed he would not have a family until his life's work was completed. Between 1863 and 1876 the *Grand dictionnaire universel* appeared in 524 parts costing one franc each. It became known simply as the 'Larousse', but the man who thus became a household name sold only 500 sets in his lifetime. He died in 1875, a year before the final volume was published – although he had by then relented in his earlier vow and married Caubel in 1872.

The fashion for encyclopaedias also inspired the development of comprehensive dictionaries. The *Oxford English Dictionary*, now commonly known by its acronym 'OED', was an epic production conceived in the 1850s when Britain was approaching the height of its global power, but not completed until 1928. Its chief proponent was Sir James A. H. Murray (1837–1915), who edited the earliest drafts of the text in a shed that he called the 'scriptorium' at Mill Hill School near London, although he did not live to see the project come to fruition. The OED was an etymological dictionary, which included a history of the usage of words – over 400,000 of them in all – in twelve weighty volumes. The information was contributed by thousands of volunteers, rather like today's Wikipedia, heroically dedicated to the spread of knowledge.

The reptile page from the *Nouveau Larousse Illustré*, volume 7. Unlike the original Larousse dictionary, this one was profusely illustrated. It was edited by Claude Augé between 1898 and 1907. It remains one of the few books named after its publisher, who had become a household name.

Modern encyclopaedias celebrated colonial power and national identity. The *Cyclopaedia of New Zealand* appeared in 1897–1908, and Australia produced its own *Australian Encyclopaedia* (1925–26), published by Angus & Robertson in Sydney and modelled on Chambers's *Cyclopaedia*. They included entries on their countries' flora and fauna and important historical figures. Similarly, the thirty-six-volume *Enciclopedia Italiana* (1929–37) celebrated the values of the Fascist government.

As the twentieth century wore on, the romance of the encyclopaedia that had once inspired committed pedagogues such as Larousse began to fade, and the national connections of the various editions were gradually severed: the *Encyclopaedia Britannica*, for instance, was sold to the American publishers Hooper & Jackson in 1901. By the end of the twentieth century, print encyclopaedias were making way for electronic versions that incorporated sound, video clips and animated graphics. Electronic encyclopaedias enjoy many advantages over their huge, multi-volume print predecessors: they cost less to produce and are easier to update. They can be searched rapidly, while hyperlinks facilitate cross-referencing.

Founded in 2001, Wikipedia offers an alternative encyclopaedia in which all entries are contributed by online readers who can freely add and correct text. ('Wikis' are web pages designed to allow group collaboration, and the name derives from the Hawaiian word for 'quick'.) Wikipedia resembles an endless palimpsest, in constant evolution, with its content perpetually verified and updated by consensus. In 2010, the English edition included over 3.3 million entries. The utopian search for universal knowledge has turned a new corner: now everybody can contribute to an encyclopaedia.

An advertisement for *Dennerts Konversationslexikon*, a popular German encyclopaedia compiled by the anti-Darwinist philosopher Eberhard Dennert (1861–1942).

Penguins and the Paperback Revolution

The paperback revolution of the mid-twentieth century is indelibly associated with Penguin Books and its visionary creator, Allen Lane (1902–70). Lane drew on the German precedent of Albatross Verlag, whose Albatross Modern Continental Library, established in 1932, issued cheap paperback reprints in colour-coded covers. By the time Lane's Penguins – imitating their German predecessor's seabird motif – were launched in Britain in 1935, Albatross had already published 272 volumes in their series.

Lane had immediate competition: Collins had launched a series of 7d reprints in 1934, and Pearson started selling 6d paperback novels in 1936. But Lane's entrepreneurial gamble paid off: Penguin sold 3 million books in its first year, with a turnover of £75,000; its first bestseller was Dorothy L. Sayers's *The Unpleasantness at the Bellona Club*. Lane celebrated by buying a yacht and naming it 'Penguin'. In its first twenty years, Penguin published 1,000 titles, with a total print run of about 20 million copies annually, and by the 1950s, Penguin accounted for 7 or 8 per cent of Britain's entire book production.

Penguins were cheap – they cost only sixpence – but unlike the pulp fiction offerings then dominating the paperback market, they were reprints of high-quality texts by established literary authors, appealing to the educated reader. Like Albatross books, their rather plain covers were colour-coded: orange for fiction, green for crime, and so on. From the 1950s onwards, Penguin's instantly recognizable paperbacks generated strong sales, particularly among the growing proportion of the population that was university-educated. Authors such as D. H. Lawrence and George Orwell would each sell over a million copies in this paperback format. One measure of Lane's achievement was the string of imitators who followed his lead: Pan and Corgi in Britain, Bantam and Signet in the USA, and Hachette's *Livres de poche* in France.

The financial success of the paperback revolution lay not in the inexpensive cover and binding but in the huge economies of scale that could be achieved from long print runs. Marketing and distribution were also decisive factors

Various Penguin paperbacks with their distinctive colour-coded covers: green for crime and orange for modern fiction. Allen Lane built on a German precedent for his groundbreaking imprint.

in Penguin's success. The brand became far more important than any individual author or title.

In 1960 Lane took another calculated risk in publishing an unexpurgated version of D. H. Lawrence's *Lady Chatterley's Lover*, which had already been declared obscene in the USA (where it was published by Grove Press) for its descriptions of sexual encounters between Constance Chatterley and her gamekeeper Mellors. In England, however, the new Obscene Publications Act of 1959 had relaxed the rules, and proof of literary merit would now be allowed as a defence against obscenity if it was attested by expert witnesses from the world of literature. Lane looked in vain for a printer willing to take the risk of

producing *Lady Chatterley's Lover*, until Western Printing Services agreed to do so on condition that it was insured against all legal costs. Lane agreed, and when prosecution inevitably ensued, he mobilized a number of prominent literary experts – including the novelist E. M. Forster – to testify against the obscenity charge and was found not guilty. The trial cost Penguin £12,777, but the book sold 2 million copies before Christmas 1960, and another 1.3 million in 1961, when Penguin became a public company. Once again, Lane had dared to show the way.

Consumer Culture in Weimar Germany

Erich Maria Remarque's *Im Westen Nichts Neues* (All Quiet on the Western Front), first published by Ullstein in Berlin in 1929, was arguably Germany's first twentieth-century national bestseller, selling over 900,000 copies in its first year. Remarque's unprecedented sales were just one sign that the commercialization of German bookselling was rapidly accelerating during the interwar period. Germany had by then the largest national market for books in the West, and in 1927 boasted a production total of over 37,800 titles. Between 1875 and the 1920s the number of active booksellers and publishers in the country had tripled.

Many German intellectuals were horrified by what they viewed as the rising tide of trash and the decline of traditional book culture. In 1926 the Waldorf–Astoria cigarette company in Stuttgart produced a sixteen-page mini-book that was distributed in its cigarette packets: a clear sign to many that German literature was being fatally demeaned by crass consumerism. In 1926 the Reichstag introduced the Law for the Protection of Young People against Trash and Filth, which set up bureaux to examine books purported to be obscene. Anyone convicted of distributing forbidden works could be sent to prison for a year. Initially there were 270 convictions, but the impetus quickly went out of the movement and in 1932 there were only forty-three convictions.

Copyright and pricing changes were at the heart of the new upsurge in German book production. In 1867 copyright had been removed from the works of authors who had died before 1837, putting a number of classics into the public domain. Within fifty years, Reclam had published 18 million reprints of the works of Friedrich Schiller, Johann Gottfried von Herder, Johann Wolfgang von Goethe, Gotthold Ephraim Lessing and other German masters, not to mention almost 800,000 copies of Immanuel Kant's writings. Meanwhile, the Kröner reform of 1887 established a fixed system of retail prices for books that was set by the publishers. By the mid-1920s the *de facto* cartel of publishers was still trying to maintain the average price of a German book at over 5.5 marks, but their grip was failing: department stores sold inexpensive editions (*Volksausgaben*) costing only 2.85 marks, which were beginning to dominate the market, and book clubs

The warehouse of the German publishers Reclam, photographed in 1930. Established in Leipzig in 1828, the company put millions of cheap reprints of classical German authors on the market in its famous 'Universal Bibliothek' series.

The cover of Thomas Mann's *Buddenbrooks*, published in Berlin in 1901 by S. Fischer Verlag. It was Mann's first novel, and the story of the slow decline of a north German bourgeois family became a major success and literary classic.

(*Buchgemeinschaften*) offered substantial discounts. Between 1918 and 1933 Thomas Mann's novel *Buddenbrooks* (1901) sold over a million copies at the discounted price through the Buch-Gemeinschaft club, as sales rocketed after Mann was awarded the Nobel Prize for literature in 1929. The Communists maintained a book club, as did the Social Democrats and Protestant, Jewish and Catholic groups; the Nazis, meanwhile, had their own Brauner Buch-Ring.

When the Nazis came to power in 1933, they put a swift end to this rich diversity in the German publishing industry. Public book-burnings and widespread blacklisting forced many of the most creative writers and progressive publishers into exile.

The Romance Novel: Mills & Boon

Today romance novels are represented worldwide by a range of imprints such as Harlequin and Silhouette. But between the 1930s and the 1960s the genre was synonymous with one publisher: Mills & Boon.

Founded by British entrepreneurs Gerald Mills and Charles Boon in 1908, Mills & Boon began life as a general publisher and had early success with the novels of Jack London (1876–1916) and Gaston Leroux's *The Phantom of the Opera* (1911), but after

As evident from this 1947 cover design, romantic fiction was an important ingredient in the success of the British magazine *Woman's Own*, founded in 1932. Today it treats romance in a less stereotypical fashion.

Alan Boon and his brother Charles at the helm of Mills & Boon, established in 1908. The company became synonymous with romantic pulp fiction and still publishes around fifty titles per month.

narrowly surviving the Depression the firm started to specialize in romantic fiction aimed at a female readership. By the 1930s, Mills & Boon was producing over 160 titles a year. Commercial circulating libraries such as Boots's and W. H. Smith's helped to sustain this astonishing level of production, which was even more remarkable considering that the firm did not join the paperback revolution until the 1960s. Hundreds of unknown authors produced Mills & Boon fiction, and very few of them are remembered: they wrote to a formula and the publisher's name defined the collection. The story was always told from the perspective of the heroine, for whom motherhood and domesticity predictably beckoned. Marriage, or reconciliation between husband and wife, was the desired conclusion of every romance novel.

The genre evolved during the post-war period. In the 1960s, the romance heroine began to show more interest in pursuing an independent career, often as a nurse, and the settings of the novels grew increasingly exotic as foreign travel came within the reach of ordinary readers. The male hero, however, remained strong, handsome and generous – conceived according to the Mills & Boon 'Alphaman' formula. Faced by competition from more explicit 'bodice-rippers', Mills & Boon relaxed its ban on overt eroticism, but expletives and divorce remained taboo.

In 1971 the Canadian firm Harlequin bought Mills & Boon, and in 1984 it acquired Silhouette Books of New York. By 1998 the Harlequin conglomerate had global sales of 160 million copies in twenty-four languages. Mills & Boon had become a cog in a huge romance-churning multinational.

Mills & Boon and Harlequin covers from 1913 to the present day. Recurrent themes illustrate the success of the formula, although in more recent times it has been adapted to changing women's aspirations and weakening sexual taboos.

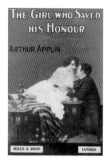

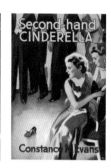

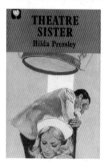

Japanese Manga

Manga account for 30 per cent of Japanese publishing output, in terms of sales volume, in both magazine and book formats. Manga are story-comics, serialized in cheap, small-format periodicals sold at bookshops, news-stands, vending machines and convenience stores. They are typically printed in black-and-white on rough or recycled pages, glued or side-stapled together and finished with an eye-catching multicoloured cover. Inside, the monochrome panels are read from top to bottom and from right to left, following the orientation of Japanese texts. Caricature, enhanced emotional states and exciting visual effects are their stock-in-trade. About a dozen popular titles sell two to three million copies weekly. *Shonen Jump* reached a record circulation of 5 million in 1988.

Manga themes are infinitely varied. They include boys' comics (*shonen manga*), girls' comics (*shojo manga*), which started in the 1960s, and comics for adults. They deal with school life, action and adventure, romance, sport, epic stories, comedy, science fiction, horror, religion and pornography as well as educational subjects. There is absolutely nothing that cannot be turned into a manga. In 1986 *Manga Nihon keizai nyomon*, a manga version of *Introduction to the Japanese Economy*, sold two million copies. Successful serials are gathered into a paperback edition, usually produced by one of the three major *manga* publishers: Kodansha, Shueisha and Shogakukan. Enthusiasts used to read their favourite episodes in twenty-four-hour manga café chains, but today they are more likely to download them to read on their mobile phones.

Manga have a long artistic pedigree. The term, which describes a series of spontaneous and disconnected drawings that stimulate the imagination, was first coined by the artist Katsushika Hokusai (1760–1849) in a compendium of his illustrations. But the dynamic gestures and exaggerated facial expressions characteristic of manga may derive from twelfth-century humorous picture scrolls (*emakimono*), and their aesthetic also owes something to the stylized expressions of traditional Kabuki theatre.

Osamu Tezuka created the manga character Astro Boy in 1952 and the robot subsequently became the hero of a successful TV series and anime film as manga fiction was adapted for different media.

Contemporary manga have been inspired by non-Japanese traditions, such as Western political cartoons and American comic strips. After the Second World War, manga incorporated cinematic techniques, but became more pessimistic, increasingly portraying scenarios in which a doomed planet, devastated by some technologically induced catastrophe, was saved by a heroic adolescent. *Mazinger Z* (1972) was one of the first to feature giant combat robots, which have since become a stock motif of the genre. In the gentler schoolgirl manga, such as *Sailor Moon* (1991–97), the heroine may have magical powers.

There is a close and symbiotic relationship between manga, anime (Japanese animation) and other modern mass-media. In 1963, for example, the internationally successful animated television series *Astro Boy* (*Tetsuwan Atomu*) first aired in Japan, one of the first regular anime series to be broadcast. It was based on a 1952 manga series of the same name by the renowned artist Osamu Tezuka (1928–89) and subsequently was made into a feature-length 3-D computer-animated film in 2009, followed by a video game. Video games now extend the impact of print-based manga, and the aesthetics and plot lines of many modern Japanese films are also influenced by the genre.

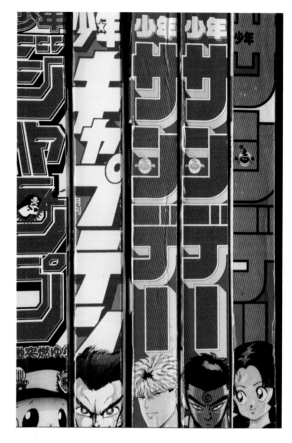

Above: Manga covers appeal to younger readers but also combine old Japanese artistic traditions with the nonstop action of Western-style comics. The spines include 'Sunday', 'Captain' and issues of 'Jump', a series published by Shueisha.

Left: A reader browses through a volume of the 'Bleach' series of manga novels (English version), involving tales of evil spirits and psychic energy. 'Bleach' has run since 2001, was serialized in *Weekly Shonen Jump* and spawned a TV series and several animated films.

The Contemporary Arab World

The Arab world comprises twenty-two countries,
stretching from Mauritania to Oman; this vast area
embraces a highly heterogeneous readership with varying
rates of literacy. The book industry in the region is
inevitably linked to each nation's wealth and stability.

In the mid-twentieth century, Cairo and Beirut
became the capitals of the Arab book market and centres
of innovation. Cairo was the first place of publication of
Nobel laureate Naguib Mahfouz (*The Cairo Trilogy*,
1956–57), playwright and short-story writer Yusuf Idris
(*The Cheapest Nights*, 1954), and female novelist Latifa al-
Zayyat (*The Open Door*, 1960). Both Cairo and Beirut invested extensively in the
translation of Western literature into Arabic. The popular saying 'Egypt writes, Lebanon
prints and Iraq reads' dates from the 1960s, and reflects Lebanon's publishing supremacy
in this period, when Beirut was an important production centre, largely because of the
Lebanese government's liberal attitude towards censorship. The independent publisher
Dar al-Adab, for example, has been in business in Beirut since 1956. It has produced
important works of Arab literature, including those of Syria's foremost novelist Hanna
Mina (born 1924), and is one of the most prestigious publishing houses in the Arab world.

Above: Naguib Mahfouz, author of
The Cairo Trilogy, is Egypt's most
widely recognized novelist. He
won the Nobel Prize for Literature
in 1988.

Left: A bookseller at his
well-stocked stand at
al-Azhar University in Cairo.

Beirut managed to maintain its leadership in book production during the civil war (1975–91), attracting Egyptian intellectuals and Syrian businessmen specializing in heritage Islamic works (*turāth*) for markets across the Arab world. Dar al-Fikr, for example, founded in 1967, publishes translations of the Koran in several African languages. Cheap *turāth* works are characterized by their imitation-leather bindings adorned with calligraphic script. In Egypt, these popular editions of Islamic classics are sold cheaply at kiosks and book markets in the al-Azhar district of Cairo. The Shi'a publishing houses of Beirut entered the Iraqi market after the fall of Saddam Hussein in 2003, setting up offices in Baghdad and Najaf. Lebanon still offers the widest range of titles in the region, including Islamic works, modern Arab literature, dictionaries, encyclopaedias and children's literature.

In 2009 Beirut was named the UNESCO World Capital of the Book, a tribute to its importance and to the strength of Lebanon's recovery from years of war. However, Beirut now faces strong competition from both its old rival Cairo and the United Arab Emirates, where book fairs have enjoyed rapid development as the university-educated population has grown. Saudi Arabia is now a major producer of Islamic books, while Syria, Jordan and the Maghreb nations are increasingly active. In these countries private publishing houses are multiplying where once the state exerted close supervision of the book trade.

A Lebanese university student browses through an Arabic novel at a Beirut bookshop in 2009 when Beirut was nominated UNESCO World Book Capital of the year. Its liberal culture makes it a leading centre of new fiction publishing in the Arab world.

The Nobel Prize for Literature

It has been accused of being narrow-minded, Eurocentric and too politicized – and yet the Nobel Prize remains the most prestigious literary prize in the world. Unlike national prizes such as the American National Book Award or the British Man Booker Prize, it does not depend on the citizenship of the author or reflect the commercial success of a recent individual title, and unlike the French Prix Goncourt, its jury members do not have close connections to leading publishing houses. They have made a few incomprehensible decisions, and also a few inspiring ones.

Upon his death, the Swedish industrialist Alfred Nobel (1833–96) bequeathed his fortune to establish annual international prizes for physics, chemistry, medicine, peace and literature. In his will he directed that the literature prize should go to someone who produced significant literary work 'with an idealistic tendency', but interpreting what that phrase really meant was problematic. In the early years of the prize it was grounds for excluding Émile Zola and Henrik Ibsen because they were considered too pessimistic, and it was difficult at first for any author who was not religious to win. Later interpretations were more relaxed and some quite pessimistic writers, such as Samuel Beckett (1969), became Nobel laureates.

At first only the Swedish Academy was permitted to present candidates for the prize, together with members of the French and Spanish Academies. The influence of French academicians voting *en bloc* probably explains the award of the very first Nobel Prize to Sully Prudhomme in 1901. The award is now decided by a committee, usually consisting of five members chosen by the Swedish Academy from its own membership, sometimes with an outside expert added. The committee's discussions are confidential, and all nominations and correspondence relating to the award are kept secret for fifty years. The prize is currently worth 10 million Swedish kronor. There have been 106 winners to date, with a few interruptions, notably in the war years of 1940–43.

Some very conservative choices were made in the early period, but many eminent writers were nevertheless recognized, including Thomas Mann (1929), Bertrand Russell (1950), Albert Camus (1957) and Jean-Paul Sartre (1964). At the same time, there have been a few celebrated losers, including Marcel Proust, Franz Kafka and Paul Valéry, who was unsuccessfully nominated twelve times. Northern European writers have historically won a disproportionate number of prizes, partly because the selection process centres on the Swedish Academy, and nearly two-thirds of winners have come from Western Europe.

Until recent years, there have been relatively few prize-winners from the developing world. The first Asian winner of the Nobel Prize for Literature was the Bengali poet Rabindranath Tagore (1913). The first South American Nobel laureate was the Chilean

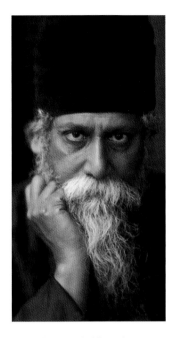

Bengali poet and philosopher Rabindranath Tagore (1861–1941) became the first Nobel laureate in literature from Asia in 1913. His best-known work, *The Home and the World*, was published in 1916.

poet Gabriela Mistral (1945). Chilean poet Pablo Neruda (1971) and Colombian novelist Gabriel García Márquez (1982) followed later. African winners have included the Nigerian novelist Wole Soyinka (1986), and South Africans Nadine Gordimer (1991) and J. M. Coetzee (2003). The first recipient from the Arab world was the Egyptian novelist Naguib Mahfouz (1988). There has been one Australian Nobel prize-winner, Patrick White (1973). Several American writers have been rewarded, starting with Sinclair Lewis in 1930, soon followed by Eugene O'Neill (1936), William Faulkner (1949), Ernest Hemingway (1954) and John Steinbeck (1962).

Political factors also influence the selection of the laureates. Leo Tolstoy, for example, was rejected because of his anarchism. The political circumstances of the Cold War also partly explained the award of the prize to Boris Pasternak (1958) and Aleksandr Solzhenitsyn (1970). Former British Prime Minister Winston Churchill received the award in 1953, a choice that was severely criticized as being politically motivated. In 2009 the prize was awarded to Herta Müller, a Romanian-born German-language novelist whose work describes daily life against the background of the Ceausescu dictatorship. As well as symbolically marking the end of the Cold War, her win illustrates the committee's present concern to give accolades to relatively unnoticed writers.

Only two winners have declined the prize: Pasternak in 1958 under pressure from the Soviet authorities, and Sartre in 1964 because he always turned down such honours.

Below left: Colombian writer Gabriel García Márquez (born 1927) holding his Nobel Prize for Literature medal after the award ceremony in Stockholm in 1982.

Below right: Romanian-born German writer Herta Müller (born 1953) was the surprise winner of the Nobel Prize for Literature in 2009. In her novels, including *The Land of Green Plums* (1993), she charted the hardships and humiliations of Nicolae Ceausescu's brutal regime.

Children's Books

The earliest books intended specifically for children were educational texts, conduct books and simple ABCs, which were frequently decorated with animals, plants and anthropomorphic letters. Until the nineteenth century, children in English-speaking countries often learned to read from a horn-book, which was a small, flat piece of wood with a short handle, holding a sheet of paper protected by a thin, transparent sheet of horn. The sheet usually contained the alphabet, a list of elementary syllables consisting of two letters each, and a prayer such as the Lord's Prayer. Early reading primers often had a frontispiece showing a child learning to read at his or her mother's knee: until the late nineteenth century, the home, not the school, was the usual environment where children acquired early literacy.

In the nineteenth century, a few children's titles became famous as classroom reading texts. Among these were the fables of Aesop and Jean de la Fontaine (1621–95), as well as many folktales, which in the early nineteenth century evolved into 'fairy tales'. Another early and influential children's collection was Charles Perrault's 1697 *Tales of Mother Goose*, credited as the book that founded the literary genre of the fairy tale as a whole.

The popularity of these early collections inspired a number of nineteenth-century fantasy and fairy tales for children that included motifs such as magic objects and talking animals. Hans Christian Andersen's *Fairy Tales*, a series of original stories for children that included modern fairy-tale classics such as *The Little Mermaid* and *The Princess and the Pea*, was published in 1835–45 and gradually became an international success. In 1865 Lewis Carroll published *Alice's Adventures in Wonderland* to immediate acclaim; Carlo Collodi's *Avventure di Pinocchio* (1886) was a bestselling serial in Italy before becoming a global favourite in book form. Even Astrid Lindgren's twentieth-

Opposite: An illustration drawn by Arthur Rackham for 'The Goblin and the Grocer', a fairy tale by Danish author Hans Christian Andersen (1805–75). The drawing appeared in the 1932 Harrap edition of Andersen's *Fairy Tales*.

Below: John Tenniel's drawings are indelibly associated with Lewis Carroll's *Alice in Wonderland*, a children's classic first published by Macmillan in 1865. In this scene the March Hare, the Dormouse and the Mad Hatter irritate Alice with their nonsense.

Pippi Longstocking, the fictional Swedish character endowed with superhuman strength, always remained nine years old and refused to grow up. After an initial rejection, author Astrid Lindgren managed to get the first *Pippi* book published in 1945 by Rabén and Sjögren.

century *Pippi Longstocking* books owed much to the fairy- and folktale genre with their comic, fantastic stories featuring a mischievous redhead who, with superhuman physical strength and unlimited wealth at her disposal, transcends the constraints of ordinary Swedish children's lives.

In the late nineteenth and early twentieth centuries, a corpus of children's novels emerged with realistic, non-magical plot lines centred on young protagonists. Internationally successful titles included Robert Louis Stevenson's *Treasure Island* (1883), L. M. Montgomery's *Anne of Green Gables* (1908) and Louisa May Alcott's *Little Women* (1869), which were translated into dozens of languages. Between 1890 and 1930, children's literature became an essential component of the book market. Publishers established children's editors, and public libraries opened rooms devoted to children's books.

Children's books are an important and lucrative market for modern publishers: twentieth-century reading surveys show that the peak reading age for males and females is about twelve or thirteen. The children's book has also been particularly successful in competing with rival media, displaying an ingenuity lacking in the more sedate world of publishing for adults. Pop-up books, books with multiple alternative endings and books with sound and texture have all interested child readers. The phenomenal success of J. K. Rowling's Harry Potter series (1997–2007), however, shows the resilience of more traditional forms of children's literature such as the fantasy/fairy-tale and school-fiction genres. The seven Harry Potter books have reportedly sold more than 400 million copies for their publisher Bloomsbury, and have been made into top-grossing films by Time Warner, leaving their stunned author a billionaire within a few years.

Children's literature has always attracted innovative illustrators whose work has been crucial in stimulating young readers' imagination. Lewis Carroll's *Alice* books, for instance, became indelibly associated with political cartoonist John Tenniel's drawings. Technological advances in illustrated book production have allowed twentieth-century illustrators to create children's books that are beautiful, colourful, richly produced works of art, ranging from Maurice Sendak's evocative *Where the Wild Things Are* to the exuberant *Meg and Mog* series of Polish-born Jan Pienkowski, who also works as a stage designer. The fantastic, unsettling worlds of Australian artist Shaun Tan go a step beyond illustrating a printed text: his illustrations for *The Lost Thing* (2000) and *Tales from Outer Suburbia* (2008) play on the theme of the inadequacy of verbal communication itself.

The Harry Potter novels are a publishing phenomenon in many languages, supported by an exceptionally thorough marketing effort by English publishers Bloomsbury and their international partners, together with film producers Warner Brothers.

Book Illustration and Design

A range of new techniques, developed during the nineteenth and twentieth centuries, revolutionized the illustration of books and put new resources at the disposal of artists and designers. In the early nineteenth century, the photogravure process first allowed photographs to be reproduced in books; light-sensitive gelatin was used to transfer the image to a metal plate, which could then be etched. Chromolithography, developed in France in the mid-nineteenth century, permitted colour printing, although the process was labour-intensive and expensive, as the artist had to prepare a separate plate for each colour. In the later twentieth century, offset lithography made colour printing cheaper and less time-consuming, using a chemical process to transfer a photographic negative

The 'Kelmscott Chaucer', showing William Morris's characteristic floral designs and use of medieval motifs typical of the Pre-Raphaelite group of painters.

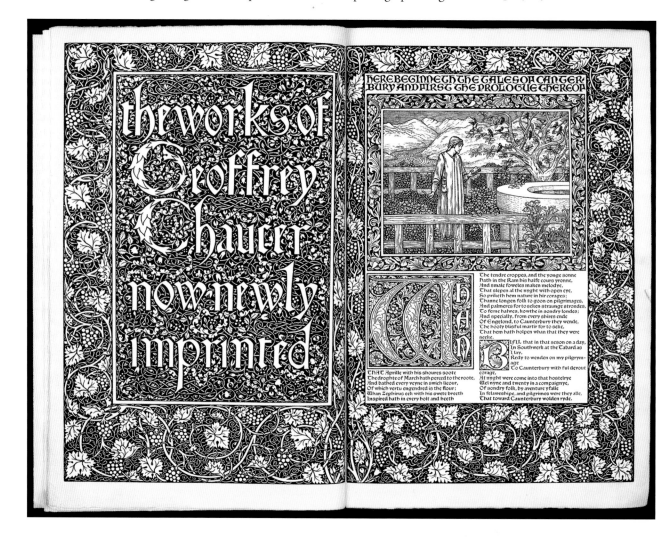

to a rubber surface before printing. Now desktop publishing software can make anyone a book illustrator or designer.

Nineteenth- and twentieth-century avant-garde artistic movements took an interest in the typographical arts, greatly enriching book design and illustration. In the late nineteenth century, William Morris (1834–96) founded the Arts and Crafts movement, which emphasized the value of traditional craft skills that seemed to be disappearing in the mass industrial age. His designs, like the work of the Pre-Raphaelite painters with whom he was associated, referred frequently to medieval motifs. In 1891 he founded the Kelmscott Press, which by the time it closed in 1898 had produced over fifty works using traditional printing methods, a hand-driven press and handmade paper. They included his masterpiece, an edition of the *Works of Geoffrey Chaucer* with illustrations by Edward Burne-Jones (1833–98). Morris invented three distinctive typefaces – Golden, Troy and Chaucer – and framed the text with intricate floral borders reminiscent of illuminated medieval manuscripts. His example inspired many small private presses in the following century.

Aubrey Beardsley (1872–98), an exponent of Art Nouveau and Aestheticism, also exerted a great influence over book illustration. He specialized in erotica, some of the best examples being his drawings for the first English edition of Oscar Wilde's *Salomé* (1894): Wilde himself thought the images eclipsed the text. Beardsley also illustrated a deluxe edition of Thomas Malory's *Le Morte d'Arthur*.

Twentieth-century avant-garde art movements such as Dadaism, surrealism and Bauhaus were also interested in book design and illustration. Unlike William Morris,

THE LADY OF THE LAKE TELLETH ARTHVR OF THE SWORD EXCALIBVR

Aubrey Beardsley's drawings for Dent's lavish edition of *Le Morte d'Arthur* (1893–94) set new standards in book illustration. Beardsley, who was part of the Art Nouveau movement, died of tuberculosis at only twenty-five.

however, they embraced the machine age, introducing many *sans sérif* fonts, which in their view represented modernism.

Kurt Schwitters (1887–1948), a German artist strongly influenced by Dadaism, experimented with typography in the years leading up to the Second World War, as did his friend El Lissitzky (1890–1941), a Russian constructivist artist and typographer whose work perhaps had a more lasting impact on his fellow artists. Lissitzky began his career illustrating Yiddish children's books, including *Had Gadya* (The Only Kid, 1919), inspired by a traditional Jewish Passover song. While working in Berlin during the early 1920s as a cultural attaché for the Soviet government, he designed a number of influential books, including a collection of poems by Vladimir Mayakovsky entitled *Dlia Golosa* (For the Voice, 1923), and *Die Kunstismen* (The Isms of Art, 1925), an art manifesto produced in collaboration with the Alsatian sculptor Jean Arp. Lissitzky frequently used Hebrew and Cyrillic lettering as an integral part of his designs. In addition to his books, he produced many Soviet propaganda posters and was also an architect, appointed by the government to design exhibition spaces.

El Lissitzky preferred to call his design work 'book construction'. Red and black ink dominate this 1923 edition of works by the avant-garde poet Vladimir Mayakovsky. On the left is a hammer and sickle and the right-hand margin is stepped like an address book to index the poems.

Illustrated Books

During the early twentieth century, many of the great names in illustrated book publishing began to emerge, including Piper, founded in Munich in 1904, Phaidon, founded in 1923 in Vienna, and Skira, founded in Lausanne in 1928. It was not until the radical improvement in the quality of four-colour offset printing from the mid-twentieth century, however, that colour photographs could be affordably reproduced in books for the mass market. These developments in printing technology transformed not only art and photography books, but also children's, cookery and travel publishing.

Despite these advances, illustrated books remain comparatively expensive to produce. Skira and Phaidon were among the first to neutralize the costs by focusing on large print runs aimed at a broad market, and by selling international co-editions: that is, foreign-language versions of their own books, produced for overseas publishers in the same print run. In 1950, for instance, Phaidon published *The Story of Art*, a popular one-volume survey of the history of art by Ernst Gombrich. Continuously in print, it has been published in over thirty languages. Co-editioning has become the model for much illustrated book publishing, and has helped to create a genuinely international publishing community.

Before the start of the Second World War, a number of talented Central European publishers fled to Britain, bringing with them a strong visual and literary culture, and a tradition of professionalism and craftsmanship in book production. Phaidon's founders, Bela Horovitz and Ludwig Goldscheider, moved the company to England following Germany's annexation of Austria in 1938. Walter Neurath, a Viennese

Ernst Gombrich was born in Austria but settled in England in 1936. Phaidon published his book *The Story of Art* in 1950, making high-quality art books available to a general public. It is claimed to be the most popular art book ever written.

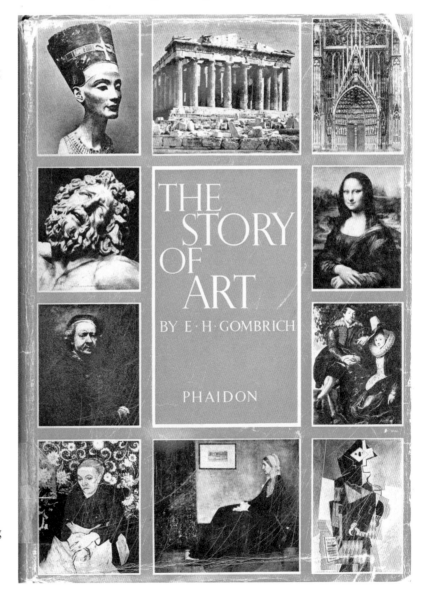

publisher, arrived in London in the same year. He was initially employed as production director at pioneering book packager Adprint, where he worked on the Britain in Pictures series made for Collins. In 1949 Neurath and Eva Feuchtwang (a fellow émigré and Adprint employee who was later to become his wife) established Thames & Hudson in London and New York. Their aim was to publish affordable books on art, sculpture and architecture that would educate and entertain non-specialist audiences.

Walter Neurath at his desk. An Austrian refugee, he founded Thames & Hudson together with his future wife to offer high-quality art books at affordable prices.

A Thames & Hudson book display at Hatchards bookshop, Piccadilly, London, in 2010.

Until the middle of the twentieth century, most art books available in America were imported from Europe. Harry N. Abrams, founded in 1949, was the first American company to specialize in the creation of richly illustrated art books. Walter Neurath initially supervised the European production of Abrams books. In 1952 Harry Abrams hired Fritz Landshoff, a German émigré publisher, and, in 1955, his son Andreas, to produce Abrams books and arrange European co-editions. Their efforts were very successful: *The Picture History of Painting* (1957) by art historian H. W. Janson, for instance, was translated into twelve languages, and a paperback series of artist's monographs was co-published by nine European publishers, selling close to 3 million copies. Harry Abrams sold his company to Times–Mirror in 1966, but continued to run it until 1977; the firm is now a subsidiary of the Paris-based La Martinière Groupe.

The Cologne-based newspaper company M. DuMont Schauberg, founded in the early seventeenth century, began publishing illustrated books in 1956, encouraged by the Landshoffs, who were close friends of the DuMonts. Characterized by high standards of authorship, design and colour reproduction, the DuMont list developed to include not only art books, but also travel guides and calendars. Other key German houses include Prestel, Hirmer and Hatje Cantz (incorporated as Verlag Gerd Hatje in 1947, which merged with Edition Cantz in 1997).

Eastern European publishers, many state-run for much of their history, have also been active in illustrated book publishing. From its foundation in Budapest in 1954, Corvina Kiadó prioritized international cooperation, publishing art and travel books simultaneously in English, German, French, Russian, Polish, Hungarian and other languages. State-run Polish publisher Arkady, established in Warsaw in 1957, was founded to produce illustrated books on art and architecture; following privatization in 1992, it launched general interest and children's lists, and continues to be a major buyer of foreign co-editions. Artia in Prague and Aurora in Leningrad (now again St Petersburg) were also major players in illustrated publishing in the region before the fall of Communism.

Paris-based publisher Flammarion, founded in 1875, has a long history of art book publishing. Éditions Gallimard, founded in Paris in 1911, is a relative newcomer to the genre, having built its reputation publishing many of the great literary authors of the modern era, including Marcel Proust, Jean-Paul Sartre, Simone de Beauvoir, James Joyce, Franz Kafka, Jack Kerouac and Michel Foucault. In recent decades Gallimard has developed an extensive programme of illustrated books including the popular Découvertes (Discoveries) series, which now comprises more than 500 volumes.

Garzanti, Rizzoli, Fabbri and Electa were the major names in post-war Italian illustrated publishing. Mondadori, established in Milan in 1907, set up an illustrated books division in the 1970s, publishing titles on history, art, natural history and popular culture.

Some illustrated book publishers specialize exclusively in the visual arts. Spanish publisher Ediciones Polígrafa, founded in 1961, focuses on the graphic work of leading artists from Spain and elsewhere. Tokyo visual and practical arts publisher Graphic-Sha,

founded in 1963, is an important Asian producer of illustrated books; nearly 25 per cent of its sales are international.

Taschen, founded by Benedikt Taschen in Cologne in 1980, publishes books on art and related topics, and is also noted for its books on erotic and fetishistic imagery. Instead of producing co-editions for foreign publishers, Taschen pioneered a new model of international publishing, producing books in-house in up to eight languages and making deals directly with major distributors in each territory. The Taschen list encompasses a wide range of formats, subjects and price levels, but its luxury titles attract important publicity; among the most prominent have been Helmut Newton's *Sumo* (1999), the largest and most expensive book produced in the twentieth century, and the 700-page *GOAT (Greatest of All Time)*, a celebration of the boxer Muhammed Ali, published in 2003.

Thanks both to advances in printing and to dynamic publishers during the twentieth century, books with copious colour illustrations have become accessible to a global audience of readers.

A visitor views art books during the opening day of the 24th Palexpo Book Fair in Geneva in 2010. The 'Salon du Livre' features publishers from all over Europe and attracts around 300 exhibitors and 125,000 visitors.

Global Media

In the last few decades, the publishing world has undergone rapid restructuring on a global scale. At the end of the 1980s, large media conglomerates began to take an interest in acquiring major publishing houses. As a result, many publishing companies have become small parts of gigantic communications businesses. The German conglomerate Bertelsmann AG, for example, owns several publishing houses, newspapers and magazines, but it also owns cinema studios, shares in television and radio networks and internet operations. In some cases the special character of previously independent publishing companies has been lost as they are absorbed into the corporate culture of their new owners.

The pace of these takeovers, mergers and sales has at times been bewildering. Larousse, the French publisher of internationally renowned encyclopaedias, used to be

Inside the Barnes & Noble bookstore at The Grove shopping mall, Los Angeles. Predictions that mega-bookstores like this would wipe out independent shops and impose cultural standardization have not come true completely.

owned by Havas, which was in turn owned by the Groupe de la Cité. In 1998 Havas was acquired by Compagnie Générale des Eaux, which was transformed into Vivendi and then Vivendi Universal. But in 2004 Havas Publications were again sold, under the name of Editis, to Hachette Livre and the De Wendel investment fund.

A woman views books for sale at only £1 in an Asda supermarket. Discount sales and the variety of retail outlets available have challenged the role of traditional bookshops.

The concentration of the publishing industry into a few massive firms has clear disadvantages. For one thing, the media conglomerates look for rapid and substantial profits. The mania for takeovers of publishing companies slowed down in the 1990s when their new owners realized that book publishing was rarely as profitable as they had anticipated, with a margin averaging only around 5 per cent. In 2003 when Ann Godoff, head of general literature publishing at Bertelsmann-owned Random House, could not deliver a 15 per cent annual profit, she was summarily sacked.

This emphasis on generating quick profits tends to favour the promotion of blockbusters, which can be financially risky for publishers. One factor in Godoff's downfall was the enormous advances worth millions of dollars that she had (unprofitably) lavished on bestselling authors such as Stephen King. Unfortunately for Godoff, King's sales slumped in 2002 when his *From a Buick 8* failed to meet expectations. The priorities of the media conglomerates make it more difficult to publish original or independent works whose commercial outcome is uncertain, and penalize sectors where sales are usually steady but slow. Many non-fiction titles, for example in history and the social sciences, are therefore jeopardized. Independent publishers have survived by cornering particular niches in the market, such as the extraordinarily successful Australian operation that produces the *Lonely Planet* travel series, although the company is now owned by BBC Worldwide.

Similar issues affect the modern bookselling industry, which, like publishing, is increasingly concentrated in a small number of extremely large and powerful conglomerates, particularly in the USA. The domination of the American bookselling market by large firms such as Barnes & Noble privileges bestsellers and titles that sell fast. Even these bookselling chains, however, can be undercut by large online discounters and supermarkets: in the USA, more copies of the final two Harry Potter volumes were sold in Wal-Mart and similar outlets than in Barnes & Noble. In Britain the collapse of the Retail Price Agreement for books in 1995 gave supermarket chains such as Tesco the opportunity to negotiate large discounts with publishers for the most popular titles. Independent booksellers survive with difficulty in this environment, although in continental Europe they are proving more resilient.

Globalization and Cultural Identity

In 1989 Pearson Longman closed down Scottish educational publisher Oliver & Boyd, even though it was making a net profit of 10 per cent – this was not enough for the conglomerate. Nations such as Scotland or Australia, which have relatively small populations and small book markets, sometimes feel that their distinctive literary cultures are under threat. These are, of course, countries within the English-speaking world, which means that they feel vulnerable to Americanization, even though they enjoy the advantage of being part of a large global market.

In continental Europe, however, linguistic and cultural diversity has prevented a bland euro-pudding from materializing in the book trade. The bestselling European authors continue to be published in various languages by a surprising mixture of small, large, specialist and trade publishers. European publishers employ editors who read a variety of languages, and between 10 and 30 per cent of people in the European Union read books in more than one language. According to Miha Kovac and Ruediger Wischenbart's data from the UK, France, Italy, Germany, Sweden, the Netherlands and Spain, the bestselling fiction author in Europe between April 2008 and March 2010 was neither American nor British, but the Swedish writer Stieg Larsson (1954–2004).

If globalization is to be resisted by local cultures, small regional publishers and independent booksellers need government support. This may come in the form of cultural subsidies or tax breaks. Books currently attract zero Value Added Tax (VAT) in the United Kingdom, Ireland, Poland and Croatia, but in Denmark readers pay the full VAT rate of 25 per cent. The Irish Arts Council is responsible for an increase in the number of children's titles produced in Ireland in the last twenty years. Canadian government programmes have caused substantial growth in the number of titles produced there and in the number of active Canadian publishers.

The phenomenal success of Swedish author Stieg Larsson's *Millennium Trilogy* has dispelled fears that authors and publishers from English-speaking countries would monopolize the global fiction market.

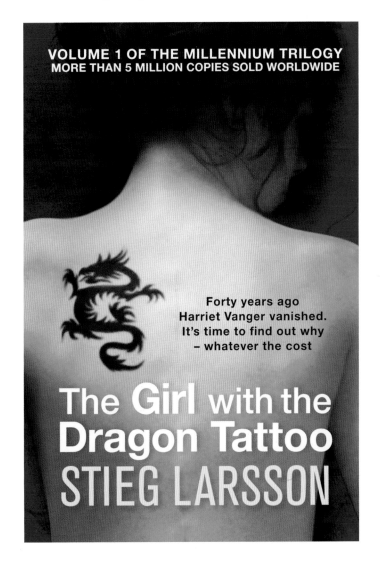

VOLUME 1 OF THE MILLENNIUM TRILOGY
MORE THAN 5 MILLION COPIES SOLD WORLDWIDE

Forty years ago Harriet Vanger vanished. It's time to find out why – whatever the cost

The Girl with the Dragon Tattoo
STIEG LARSSON

Enemies of the Book

Book-burnings have been frequent events in Europe from the Inquisition to the present day. Many regimes have attempted to contain subversive writings by publicly destroying forbidden books and punishing those who write, print and read them.

The urge to burn books has manifested itself throughout the twentieth century. The United States Postal Service burned copies of James Joyce's *Ulysses* in the 1920s. Nazi book-burnings, orchestrated by the Third Reich from 1933 onwards, aimed to cleanse German culture not merely of Jewish authors, but of all foreign influences, as well as of pacifist and decadent literature of the Weimar Republic. In Paris a group of anti-Fascist exiles set up the Library of Burned Books, containing copies of all the titles Hitler destroyed. The Nazis also seized millions of books in the Jewish centres of eastern Europe, but preserved a few rare and ancient volumes, intending to house them in a

In the presence of members of the public and high officials of the National Socialist Party, over 12,000 books of Jewish and Marxist literature were burnt by the Hitler Youth in April 1938 on the Residenzplatz in Salzburg, Austria.

Russian author Aleksandr Solzhenitsyn portrayed in 1953, when he was a prisoner at Kok-Terek in Kazakhstan. His subsequent books on the evils of Stalin's prison camp system were banned in the USSR.

museum of Judaism once the Final Solution was complete. Some of these books therefore survived the war and found their way to Israel and the USA after 1945.

In the USSR, book production was highly regulated by the state, and private publishers were not permitted to operate after 1930. The Communist Party assumed the role of defending political orthodoxy in print, and library contents were purged. Although Aleksandr Solzhenitsyn's *One Day in the Life of Ivan Denisovich* (1962) was published in the USSR during a brief period of reform under Nikita Khrushchev, his subsequent major works were suppressed for their frank portrayal of repression under the Communist regime. Solzhenitsyn (1918–2008) was expelled from the Soviet Writers' Union in 1970, and deported in 1974 after *The Gulag Archipelago* was published in the West. In the 1970s and 1980s, forbidden books could be bought in the USSR on the black market, and banned dissident authors celebrated in the West secretly circulated mimeographed copies of their works. In the era of *perestroika* inaugurated by Mikhail Gorbachev in the late 1980s, censorship was relaxed.

Censorship was not confined to totalitarian dictatorships. Until the 1960s, when a wave of literary liberation swept the West, the dead hand of Puritanism prevented the publication of many literary masterpieces that were considered sexually deviant or too explicit. D. H. Lawrence's *Lady Chatterley's Lover* (1928) first appeared in Florence, Italy, and could not be published in England until 1960, although Inky Stephensen's Mandrake Press produced an underground edition in 1929. During the 1960s, other banned works became available after years of oblivion. An American legal ruling of 1964 cleared Henry Miller's *Tropic of Cancer* (first published in Paris in 1934) of obscenity. Vladimir Nabokov's *Lolita*, which portrayed a middle-aged man's affair with a twelve-year-old girl, was finally published in America by G. P. Putnam's Sons in 1958, and in Britain by Weidenfeld & Nicolson in 1959; it had first been published in Paris in 1955 (and banned shortly thereafter), as no publisher in an English-speaking country would touch it. *Lolita* became an immediate global bestseller and, like *Lady Chatterley's Lover*, remains one of those novels that is exceptionally well known by people who have never read it.

Despite the relaxation of state censorship in many parts of the world, book-burning has not gone out of fashion in the modern age. In an attempt to destroy Bosnian culture, the National Library of Sarajevo was obliterated by Serbian shells in 1992. In Bradford, England, in 1989, Muslim demonstrators symbolically burned copies of Salman Rushdie's *Satanic Verses* (1988) for the television cameras, in protest at what they considered its blasphemous content. Even with the subsequent widening power of the internet and the rise of digitization, books are still considered important enough to burn.

A scene from 1989 showing British Muslims in Bradford, northern England, burning copies of Salman Rushdie's *Satanic Verses*, which they regarded as blasphemous in its references to the prophet Mohammed.

A UN soldier stands among the rubble of the National Library of Sarajevo, bombed by Serbia in 1992 in order to destroy the cultural heritage of Bosnia.

The Virtual Book

In the mid-nineteenth century, the book trade evolved a business model, underpinned by a royalty system and international copyright protection, that gave authors, publishers and booksellers a reasonable return for their creative labour and provided readers with ever-cheaper books. But by the end of the twentieth century, advances in electronic publishing began to bring this tried-and-trusted system into question.

Print on Demand (POD) publications have changed the traditional bookselling model. In 2007 the first so-called Espresso Machine was installed in the central branch of the New York Public Library, not to dispense coffee, but to deliver paperbacks on demand, printed from a computer file and bound in a single operation. POD machines are now commonplace in large bookshops. They eliminate distribution costs and relieve publishers and booksellers of the burden of unsold stock. This 'sell and produce' model is especially well-suited to niche markets, such as poetry and academic dissertations, which typically have very small print runs. It is less profitable for bestselling titles, as POD books are relatively expensive per unit compared to print editions.

The successful business model realized in the late nineteenth century produced benefits for all book-trade participants, but an acceptable replacement has yet to emerge in the new publishing and writing conditions of the digital age. Publishers are adapting to a new economic environment in which hand-held electronic book-reading devices such as Amazon's Kindle and the Apple iPad are becoming increasingly user-friendly and

The Espresso Machine was first installed in the New York Public Library in 2007. It produces bound paperbacks on demand in a few minutes directly from a PDF. Print on Demand is attractive for out-of-print titles or those with small specialist readership.

widespread, at the expense of some segments of the printed book market. Thanks to the internet, the second-hand book market is now global and easily accessible, which also eats into sales of new books.

Newspapers have already been irrevocably changed by the internet. Their own websites now disseminate news long before customers can read it in print. The classified ads have migrated to eBay and similar sites, while much local information is now provided by blogs and bulletin boards. Music publishing has also been transformed: digital downloads increasingly outsell CDs. But books are different, partly because they never relied on advertising income, and also because it is not quite as comfortable or convenient to read long texts on screen as it is to read a short article on a website or listen to an electronic music download on an MP3 player.

The Rise and Rise of Digitization

The advance of digitization now seems unstoppable. In the USA, e-books accounted for 2 per cent of book output in 2008–9 – admittedly not a very high proportion of the total, but increasing rapidly. Four million electronic reading devices were sold worldwide in 2009. According to American market predictions, 12 million will be sold in 2010 and perhaps 18 million in 2012. By 2015 China is expected to become the world's largest single market for e-readers, although there is still little domestic content available in China and most Chinese e-readers download books illegally.

In 2004, Google launched a project to digitize 15 million books held in American libraries and make them available for public access, creating a virtual library more vast than anything conceived at ancient Alexandria. Google Books now offers about 10 million books in digitized form. Of these, 1.5 million can be read for free, another 2 million depend on agreements with authors and publishers, and 6.5 million are under copyright and therefore only published in extracts. Google's headlong plunge into large-

E-readers like Amazon's Kindle can store several thousand books. They are lightweight, do not consume paper and can be used in poor light. However, unlike physical books they need battery power and can break if dropped.

Google Books have digitized thousands of books in partnership with many of the world's leading libraries. Neither copyright concerns nor unease about Google's monopolistic role have slowed down this massive project to scan the world's books for public access.

scale digitization has incurred legal problems: in 2005, a group of authors and publishers brought a class-action suit against Google for breach of copyright. A settlement reached in 2009 forced Google to compensate content providers – but this judgment will only apply to books in English. In France, Google may be forced to pay damages to French publishers for copyright violations.

Digitization has already changed the form of books themselves and the way they are used. In 2009 Dutton (an imprint of Penguin Group USA) published 'the world's first digi-novel', *Level 26*, a thriller by Anthony Zuiker, writer of the successful television crime series CSI. After every twenty pages, the reader encountered a code that gave internet access to a short film, which carried the story further before returning the reader to the published text. In a recent pilot project, Princeton University supplied selected students with a Kindle e-reader and issued all of their course materials electronically as a paper-saving measure. The students appreciated not having to photocopy materials or carry heavy bags of books around the campus, but they found the need to keep charging the Kindle annoying, and reported that they missed flipping through the physical book and could not highlight or annotate the text.

Millions of electronic books are now available to an infinite number of readers, but there is no guarantee that the technology of digitization will survive. Like so many technologies before it, it too could become obsolete, and the world's greatest e-libraries rendered effectively inaccessible. The digital universe is nevertheless a fact of life. In the space of a few years, books have been cut free from their paper moorings. The electronic age has changed them more fundamentally than the invention of the codex or the advent of printing.

Conclusion: The New Age of the Book

The story of the book is one of ever-widening access to reading and writing. Instead of hierarchical societies in which a privileged few had exclusive control of knowledge and information, we live today in a world of mass literacy in which ordinary people are deluged with textual information. The ascent of literacy, and with it the book, has not always been smooth: there have been many interruptions and setbacks, for instance, during the Industrial Revolution, when expanding cities imported illiteracy from the countryside, just as today Western cities import low levels of literacy from the developing world.

In 1900, print stood supreme as the universal and unrivalled medium of communication. This was the golden age of print culture: in Western society, the majority of people were literate, and the book was as yet unchallenged by radio, television or cinema. The electronic media of our own time were still a utopian dream or, more often, a sinister futuristic nightmare. This golden age of print lasted little more than a generation. In the modern digital age, the book appears to be in crisis to some

Opposite: **A book display at the Frankfurt Book Fair, which attracts 7,000 exhibitors and a quarter of a million visitors annually. Medieval booksellers used to exchange goods here; now international publishing deals and licensing agreements are negotiated at the fair.**

Left: **A book left face down in the sun. Some book lovers would deplore such casual treatment of an object that should be cherished and protected.**

An Ecuadorian woman reads a book and simultaneously listens to music in a café. Today's readers are multi-taskers who spread their attention across several media at once.

observers, who predict its impending obsolescence and incite periodic panics about declining standards of literacy.

But is there really a crisis of the book? The book industry is producing more and more titles each year, and the astronomical quantity of paper the world consumes requires stricter management of our forests. By 2005, China, the USA and the UK were each producing over 120,000 new titles annually, with the UK topping the list at over 200,000; Japan alone produces 40,000 titles every year, and the number is rising. Self-publishing is also growing exponentially. On this evidence, reports of the impending death of the book would seem to be greatly exaggerated.

As for print culture more generally, this is far from extinct. Twenty-first-century readers are not necessarily reading only books: they consume magazines, DIY manuals and a host of assorted online content as well. Young people, so often denigrated as non-readers, are simply reading differently than previous generations. They surf the web, reading large numbers of short interconnected texts rather than single extended narratives; when they do read books, they often listen to music at the same time. Books are only one option out of a number of different entertainment media available to them.

The book has survived, but at the price of its unquestioned status as an artefact of high culture. In the eighteenth century, readers would complain to the publisher if a book was poorly made, or if the printer had left an inky thumb-print on the page. Although many fine books are produced today, such connoisseurship has no place in the arena of standardized mass production and cheap, widely available paperbacks. One expression of this is that people are less respectful of the physical integrity of ordinary books than they would have been in times past. As an elderly Australian reader, Daisy B., recently told an interviewer: 'We were taught right from being very small children to look after books… We'd never think of tearing a book or leaving it lying down outside or anything like that.' A visitor to any Sydney beach on a summer Sunday afternoon will see dozens of books baking in the sun, splashed with seawater or lying face-down in the sand. The book has been dethroned, but it is part of everyday life as never before.

The so-called 'crisis of the book' is often, in fact, a crisis of the Western canon in disguise. Up until the mid-twentieth century, when a publisher decided to produce a series of national classics, there was broad agreement on which authors should be included. The last sixty years have seen the steady erosion of the old accepted cultural hierarchies – throwing off the unquestioned authority of 'dead white males'. As a consequence, the twenty-first-century literary canon is much less clearly delineated, but includes a far wider range of voices. Those who claim the book is in crisis are often those who most fervently lament the disappearance of traditional cultural hierarchies.

All these are problems of affluent Western cultures. Anxious debates about the death of the printed book are rarely heard in Africa or South America, where illiteracy rates are

A bookseller arranges his stall in Mumbai, December 2006.

much higher and access to computers and digital books is extremely limited. The world's illiteracy rate is roughly steady at about 20 per cent, but with a growing population, the number of illiterate people in the world is also growing. Some 776 million adults lack minimum literacy skills, according to UNESCO, two-thirds of them women. Illiteracy is widespread and increasing in sub-Saharan Africa and the Middle East. Literacy campaigns in the developing world, especially among women, are at the core of efforts to improve lives, linked to increased economic productivity and opportunity, improved nutrition and health, and reduced child mortality. In the absence of reliable electricity supplies in these areas, let alone computers and broadband, all the benefits of the traditional technology of the book remain paramount: it is portable, durable and reusable, and it needs no batteries or maintenance or subscription payments of any kind.

In the West, we may welcome or lament the fact that, as far as book-reading is concerned, there are no rules any more. Elsewhere in the world, the need to widen the availability of books and the skills to read them remains an enormous challenge for the decades to come.

Above: A literacy class in South Africa. Reducing illiteracy in the developing world is a continuing challenge and an urgent necessity for global progress.

Opposite: Desks and computer terminals inside the Bibliotheca Alexandrina, inaugurated in 2002, where a state-of-the-art Egyptian cultural centre pays homage to the greatest library of antiquity.

Glossary

Antiphonal
A book containing the responses sung or recited in a Christian service of worship.

apocrypha
Texts that, because of doubtful authenticity, do not form part of a canonical sacred book such as the Bible.

bibliothèque bleue
The corpus of French chapbooks, named after the blue sugar-wrapping paper in which they were often bound.

boustrophedon
A text running alternately from left to right, then right to left, resembling the path of an ox ploughing a field.

broadsheet
A large-format, single-page publication sold in the street, usually combining a woodcut image and a text such as a ballad, a polemical message or an account of a remarkable event.

chancery hand
A form of cursive handwriting for administrative and business use, first developed in the Vatican and used in regional variations throughout Europe from the thirteenth to the nineteenth century.

chapbook
An inexpensive publication produced for lower-class readers, typically between four and twenty-four pages long, printed on rough paper with crude woodcut illustrations.

codex
The modern form of the book, consisting of individual leaves bound together on one side, usually on the left (*plural:* codices).

colophon
The imprint or signature of the author, printer or publisher, sometimes decorated, on the title page of a printed book, or the signature of the scribe at the end of a handwritten manuscript.

cuneiform
The ancient script of Sumer, formed by pressing wooden wedges into soft clay.

duodecimo (in-12o)
A book format achieved by folding a full sheet to produce 12 leaves and 24 pages, and a book size of approximately 19 × 13 cm (7 × 5 in.) (*see also* folio, quarto, octavo, octodecimo).

folio
The largest book format, achieved by folding a sheet once, to produce two leaves and four pages of variable size, approximately 48 × 30 cm (19 × 12 in.) (*see also* duodecimo, quarto, octavo, octodecimo).

forme
A component of the printing press, the frame in which the galleys were laid for printing on a flat stone or slab.

galley
A tray for setting type by hand, from which galley proofs were printed.

genizah
A store of sacred Hebrew documents that have become redundant but cannot be destroyed for religious reasons.

Gothic novel
A fiction genre popular at the end of the eighteenth century, exploiting motifs such as castles, dungeons, torture and ghosts for melodramatic effect.

Gradual
A book containing music and responses for the celebration of the Mass.

incunabula
All known printed books produced before 1501 (*singular: incunabulum*).

lithography
A printing process invented in the late eighteenth century, used especially by newspapers, in which a design is drawn directly on to a smooth stone or metal printing plate, which is then treated with a chemical solution that causes the background to repel the printing ink (*see also* offset lithography).

minuscule and majuscule
Two forms of scribal handwriting, using lower-case and upper-case characters, respectively.

missal
A liturgical book containing the order and texts of different forms of the Mass.

octavo (in-8o)
A book format achieved by folding a full sheet three times, to produce eight leaves and sixteen pages approximately 23 × 15 cm (9 × 6 in.) in size (*see also* duodecimo, folio, quarto, octodecimo).

octodecimo (in-18o)

A small book format, much favoured for nineteenth-century novels, achieved by folding a full sheet to produce eighteen leaves and 36 pages approximately 16 × 10 cm (6 ½ × 4 in.) in size (*see also* duodecimo, folio, quarto, octavo).

offset lithography

A modern method of colour printing that uses a chemical process to transfer a photographic negative to a rubber surface (*see also* lithography).

palimpsest

A reused writing surface on which previous compositions have been erased and overwritten.

papyrus

The earliest form of paper, manufactured in Egypt from the pressed fibres of a marsh plant and exported throughout the Mediterranean.

parchment

A durable writing surface made from dried, scraped and bleached animal hides, used widely throughout the late Roman and medieval worlds.

pecia system

A late-medieval scribal practice by which sections of the same manuscript were contracted to different copyists, possibly laymen working for a salary.

platen

A component of the printing press, a heavy flat slab lowered to press the sheet of paper against the inked type.

pliegos sueltos

Spanish chapbook literature, literally 'loose sheets', folded into small booklets.

quarto (in-4o)

A book format achieved by folding a full sheet twice to produce four leaves and eight pages approximately 30 × 24 cm (12 × 9 ½ in.) in size (*see also* duodecimo, folio, octavo, octodecimo).

quill

A pen made from the sharpened wing-feather of a bird, usually a goose or swan.

recto and verso

The front and reverse sides of a page, respectively.

roman-feuilleton

A type of serialized fiction published in nineteenth-century French newspapers.

royalties

An author's contracted percentage of a book's earned receipts, based on the number of copies sold.

rubric

A title or subheading printed in red ink; hence also 'rubrication', the decoration in red of initial capital letters of a manuscript or printed book.

scriptio continua

A continuous script used in ancient Greece and Rome, usually in upper case throughout, without word separation, punctuation or line breaks.

scriptorium

An area, usually in a monastery, devoted to writing and copying texts.

stele

An upright stone carrying an inscription; for instance, a gravestone (*plural:* stelae).

sutra

A brief pithy statement in Hindu or Buddhist religious literature, usually gathered into collections.

three-decker novel

A novel produced in three volumes to maximize its circulation in eighteenth- and nineteenth-century libraries.

uncial

A form of early-medieval handwriting, using rounded, separated upper-case characters.

vellum

A high-grade parchment made from calfskin that has been dried, cleaned, scraped and polished.

verso

See recto and verso.

volumen

A traditional book in the form of a scroll.

xylography

An early method of woodblock printing, in which the image is carved into the wood by gouging out the areas that will not carry ink.

Further Reading

Altick, Richard D., *The English Common Reader: A social history of the mass reading public, 1800–1900* (Chicago: Chicago University Press, 1957).

Barbier, Frédéric, *L'Empire du livre: Le Livre imprimé et la construction de l'Allemagne contemporaine, 1815–1914* (Paris : Cerf, 1995).

Bechtel, Guy, *Gutenberg et l'invention de l'imprimerie: une enquête* (Paris: Fayard, 1992).

Bell, Bill, David Finkelstein and Alistair McCleery, *The Edinburgh History of the Book in Scotland*, vols. 3 and 4, (Edinburgh: Edinburgh University Press, 2007).

Blasselle, Bruno, *Histoire du livre*, 2 vols. (Paris: Gallimard/Découverte, 1997–98).

Bollème, Geneviève, *La Bibliothèque bleue: Littérature populaire en France du 17e au 19e siècle* (Paris: Julliard, 1971).

Brooks, Jeffrey, *When Russia Learned to Read: Literacy and popular literature, 1861–1917* (Princeton: Princeton University Press, 1985).

Capp, Bernard, *Astrology and the Popular Press: English almanacs, 1500–1800* (London: Faber & Faber, 1979).

Cavallo, Guglielmo and Roger Chartier, eds, *A History of Reading in the West* (Cambridge: Polity, 1999).

Chartier, Roger, *The Order of Books: Readers, authors and libraries in Europe between the 14th and the 18th centuries* (Cambridge: Polity, 1993).

Chartier, Roger and Henri-Jean Martin, eds, *Histoire de l'édition française*, 4 vols., edited in collaboration with Jean-Pierre Vivet (Paris: Promodis/Cercle de la Librairie, 1982–86; revised edition Paris: Fayard, 1989–91).

Darnton, Robert, *The Business of Enlightenment: A publishing history of the* Encyclopédie *1775–1800* (Cambridge, Massachusetts: Belknap, 1979).

Darnton, Robert, *The Forbidden Best-Sellers of Pre-Revolutionary France* (New York: W. W. Norton, 1995).

Darnton, Robert, *The Case for Books: Past, present and future* (New York: Public Affairs Books, 2009).

Davidson, Cathy N., *Revolution and the Word: The rise of the novel in America* (New York: Oxford University Press, 1986).

Eisenstein, Elizabeth L., *The Printing Revolution* (Cambridge: Cambridge University Press, 1983).

Eliot, Simon and Jonathan Rose, eds, *A Companion to the History of the Book* (Oxford: Blackwell, 2007).

Febvre, Lucien and Henri-Jean Martin, *The Coming of the Book: The impact of printing, 1450–1800* (London: New Left Book Club, 1976).

Finkelstein, David and Alistair McCleery, eds, *The Book History Reader* (London and New York: Routledge, 2002).

Fishburn, Matthew, *Burning Books* (Basingstoke: Palgrave Macmillan, 2008).

Fleming, Patricia L. et al, eds, *History of the Book in Canada*, 3 vols. (Toronto: University of Toronto Press, 2004).

Flint, Kate, *The Woman Reader, 1837–1914* (Oxford: Clarendon Press, 1993).

Furet, Francois and Jacques Ozouf, *Reading and Writing: Literacy in France from Calvin to Jules Ferry* (Cambridge: Cambridge University Press/Maison des Sciences de l'Homme, 1982).

Goody, Jack, ed., *Literacy in Traditional Societies* (Cambridge: Cambridge University Press, 1968).

Graff, Harvey, ed., *Literacy and Social Development in the West: A reader* (Cambridge: Cambridge University Press, 1981).

Gravett, Paul, *Manga: Sixty years of Japanese comics* (London: Laurence King, 2004).

Hall, David D., *Cultures of Print: Essays in the history of the book* (Amherst, Massachusetts: University of Massachusetts Press, 1996).

Hall, David D., ed., *A History of the Book in America*, 5 vols. (Cambridge: Cambridge University Press, 2000–; Chapel Hill, University of North Carolina Press, published in association with the American Antiquarian Society, 2000–).

Hofmeyr, Isabel, *The Portable Bunyan: A transnational history of* The Pilgrim's Progress (Princeton: Princeton University Press, 2004).

Houston, Robert A., *Literacy in Early Modern Europe: Culture and education, 1500–1800* (London: Longman, 1992).

Infantes, Víctor, François Lopez and Jean-François Botrel, eds, *Historia de la Edición y de la Lectura en España, 1472–1914* (Madrid: Fundación Germán Sánchez Ruipérez, 2003).

Johns, Adrian, *The Nature of the Book: Print and Knowledge in the Making* (Chicago: Chicago University Press, 1998).

Kaestle, Carl F. et al, *Literacy in the United States: Readers and Reading since 1880* (New Haven: Yale University Press, 1991).

Kornicki, Peter, *The Book in Japan: A cultural history from the beginnings to the 19th century* (Leiden: Brill, 1998).

Kovac, Miha, *Never Mind the Web: Here Comes the Book* (Oxford: Chandos, 2008).

Lovell, Stephen, *The Russian Reading Revolution: Print culture in the Soviet and post-Soviet eras* (Basingstoke: Macmillan, 2000; New York: St. Martin's Press, 2000).

Lowry, Martin, *The World of Aldus Manutius: Business and scholarship in Renaissance Venice* (Ithaca, New York: Cornell University Press, 1979).

Lyons, Martyn, *Le Triomphe du Livre: Une Histoire sociologique de la lecture dans la France du 19e siècle* (Paris: Promodis/Cercle de la Librairie, 1987).

Lyons, Martyn, *Readers and Society in Nineteenth-Century France: Workers, Women, Peasants* (Basingstoke and New York: Palgrave, 2001).

Lyons, Martyn, John Arnold, Craig Munro and Robyn Sheahan-Bright, eds, *A History of the Book in Australia*, vols. 2 and 3 (St Lucia, Queensland, Australia: University of Queensland Press, 2001–6).

Manguel, Alberto, *A History of Reading* (London: HarperCollins, 1986).

Martin, Henri-Jean, *The History and Power of Writing*, trans. Lydia G. Cochrane (Chicago: Chicago University Press, 1994) [French orig., *Histoire et pouvoirs de l'écrit* (Paris: Perrin, 1988)].

McAleer, Joseph, *Popular Reading and Publishing in Britain, 1914–50* (Oxford: Clarendon Press, 1992).

McKenzie, D. F., *Bibliography and the Sociology of Texts* (Cambridge: Cambridge University Press, 1999 and 2004).

McKenzie, D. F., D. J. McKitterick and I. R. Willison, eds, *The Cambridge History of the Book in Britain*, 7 vols. (Cambridge: Cambridge University Press, 1999–)

Mollier, Jean-Yves, *L'Argent et les lettres: Histoire et capitalisme d'édition, 1880–1920*, (Paris: Fayard, 1988).

Monaghan, E. Jennifer, *Learning to Read and Write in Colonial America* (Amherst, Massachusetts: University of Massachusetts Press, 2005).

Patten, Robert L., *Charles Dickens and his Publishers* (Oxford: Clarendon Press, 1978).

Pedersen, Johannes, *The Arabic Book* (Princeton: Princeton University Press, 1984).

Reuveni, Gideon, *Reading Germany: Literature and Consumer Culture in Germany before 1933* (New York: Berghahn, 2006).

Rose, Jonathan, *The Intellectual Life of the British Working Classes* (New Haven: Yale University Press, 2001).

St. Clair, William, *The Reading Nation in the Romantic Period* (Cambridge: Cambridge University Press, 2004).

Spufford, Margaret, *Small Books and Pleasant Histories: Popular fiction and its readership in 17th-century England* (Cambridge: Cambridge University Press, 1981).

Thomas, Rosalind, *Literacy and Orality in Ancient Greece* (Cambridge: Cambridge University Press, 1993).

Tsien, Tsuen-Hsuin, *Written on Bamboo and Silk*, 2nd edition with an afterword by Edward L. Shaughnessy (Chicago: Chicago University Press, 2004).

Turi, Gabriele, ed., *Storia dell'editoria nell'Italia contemporanea* (Florence: Giunti, 1997).

Waquet, Françoise, *Latin, or The Empire of a Sign from the 16th to the 20th Centuries* (London: Verso, 2001).

Illustration Credits

a=above, b=below, l=left, r=right

Advertising Archives 177; akg-images 103, 114r, 127, 145, 151, 169a, 176; akg-images/Archives CDA/St-Genès 113; akg-images/Cameraphoto 35b; akg-images/Electa, 26; akg-images/Imagi Animation Studios/Imagi 180; akg-images/Imagno/Anonym 175; akg-images/Erich Lessing 11, 14, 54-55, 107, 108b; akg-images/North Wind Picture Archives 152; The Art Archive/Alamy 28; Mary Evans Picture Library/Alamy 165; Tony French/Alamy 181b; Hemis/Alamy 212; Interfoto/Alamy 99, 111; Richard Levine/Alamy 206; NetPics/Alamy 207; Optikat/Alamy 181a; Pictorial Press Ltd./Alamy 201; Serdar/Alamy 197; TAO Images Limited/Alamy 34; Nik Taylor/Alamy 198; Rijksprentenkabinet, Amsterdam 106; Museum Plantin-Moretus, Antwerp 82a; Associated Press 200; Agora Museum, Athens 25b; Institute of Archaeology, CASS, Beijing 18, 19; Courtesy The Lilly Library, Indiana University, Bloomington 62, 63; Staatsbibliothek Bremen 40; Bridgeman Art Library 83; Ashmolean Museum, University of Oxford/Bridgeman Art Library 96; Bibliothèque Nationale de France, Paris/Bridgeman Art Library 75; Christie's Images/Bridgeman Art Library 97; Musée Carnavalet, Paris/Archives Charmet/Bridgeman Art Library 89; Nordiska Museet, Stockholm/Bridgeman Art Library 98; Private Collection/Agnew's, London/Bridgeman Art Library 89; Private Collection/Archives Charmet/Bridgeman Art Library 130; Parker Library, Corpus Christi College, Cambridge 41; National Library of Australia, Canberra 74, 137; State Museum, Cetinje 128; Musée Condé, Chantilly 46; Corbis 125, 172; Tony Anderson/Corbis 209; Fabrizio Bensch/Reuters/Corbis 185r; Bettmann/Corbis 142, 185l; Walter Bibikow/Corbis 149; Stefano Blanchetti/Corbis 138; Christie's Images/Corbis 126; Pascal Deloche/Godong/Corbis 52r; Macduff Everton/Corbis 12; Yves Gellie/Corbis 27b; Thomas Hartwell/Sygma/Corbis 182a; Lindsay Hebberd/Corbis 13; Historical Picture Archive/Corbis 143; E.O. Hoppé/Corbis 184; Hulton-Deutsch/Corbis 174b; Georges de Keerle/Sygma/Corbis 203; Anuruddha Lokuhapuarachchi/Reuters/Corbis 211; John Lund/Marc Romanelli/Blend Images/Corbis 210; David Pollack/Corbis 150; Qi Heng/Xinhua Press/Corbis 205; Hans Georg Roth/Corbis 166; Leonard de Selva/Corbis 33; Sygma/Corbis 202; Martial Trezzini/epa/Corbis 196; K.M. Westermann/Corbis 182b; Sächsische Landesbibliothek – Staats- und Universitätsbibliothek, Dresden 84; Trinity College, Dublin 43, 44; University Library, Michigan State University, East Lansing 79r; National Library of Scotland, Edinburgh 76l; Mary Evans Picture Library 148a; Illustrated London News Ltd/Mary Evans Picture Library 104; Joseph Barrack/AFP/Getty Images 185; Thomas Lohnes/AFP/Getty Images 208; Leon Neal/AFP/Getty Images 204; Pressens Bild/AFP/Getty Images 188; City Press/Gallo Images/Getty Images 213; Peter Macdiarmid/Getty Images 189; Niedersächsische Staats- und Universitätsbibliothek Göttingen 78a; Hereford Cathedral 39; Ironbridge Gorge Museum Trust, Ironbridge 131, 132; Israel Antiquities Authority, Jerusalem 50; British Library, London 20, 23, 24, 36, 38, 45, 49a, 52l, 53, 57b, 58, 59, 62, 65, 66, 68, 70, 77, 81, 82a, 110, 112, 164, 190, 191; British Museum, London 16, 17, 21, 25a, 31r, 69, 90, 102, 105, 117, 124, 125b, 144, 148b; Museum of London 100b; The National Archives, London 37; St. Bride's Printing Library, London 122; Musée des Beaux-Arts, Lyons 9; Biblioteca Nacional, Madrid 121r; Gutenberg Museum, Mainz 57a; John Paul Getty Museum, Malibu 35a; State Library of Victoria, Melbourne 160; Museo Archeologico Nazionale, Naples 5; Library of the Jewish Theological Seminary of America, New York 51; Germanisches Nationalmuseum, Nuremberg 22; Bodleian Library, University of Oxford, Oxford 85; Oxford University Press, Oxford 170a; Archives Hachette, Paris 174a; Bibliothèque de l'Assemblée Nationale, Paris 86; Bibliothèque Nationale de France, Paris 32, 42, 48, 49b, 67, 87l, 100a, 125a; Musée Carnavalet, Paris 132; Musée du Louvre, Paris 108a; © 1950 Phaidon Press Limited, www.phaidon.com 193; Národní knihovna České republiky, Prague 71b; Private Collection 158, 159; RMN/Gérard Blot 6, 121l; Photo Scala, Florence/Fotografica Foglia – courtesy of the Ministero Beni e Att. Culturali 29; Metropolitan Museum of Art/Art Resource/Scala, Florence 27a; © Thames & Hudson Limited 194; Christopher Simon Sykes/TIA Digital Ltd. 2-3; Tokugawa Art Museum, Tokugawa 30; National Library, Tunis 47; Library of Congress, Washington, D.C., 31l, 71a, 80, 129r, 161, 162.

Index